OVERHEARD IN DUBLIN AGAIN

DUBLIN WIT FROM
OVERHEARDINDUBLIN.COM

Gill & Macmillan

Dedicated to Phyllis

Gill & Macmillan Ltd
Hume Avenue, Park West, Dublin 12
with associated companies throughout the world
www.gillmacmillan.ie
© Gerard Kelly and Sinéad Kelly 2007
978 07171 4204 1

Print origination by TypeIT, Dublin
Illustrations by Eoin Coveney
Printed and bound by Nørhaven Paperback A/S,
Denmark

This book is typeset in 10pt Garamond Book on 11pt.

The paper used in this book comes from the wood pulp
of managed forests. For every tree felled, at least one
tree is planted, thereby renewing natural resources.

A CIP catalogue record for this book is available from
the British Library.

5 4 3 2

Spelling it out

In Ireland we have this weird habit of spelling words out loud when children are present, so that they don't understand us, you know, like, 'I'll call ya later when the child is in B-E-D.'

Well, I was in McDonald's a couple of weeks ago and a couple and their daughter were at the counter ordering. The husband orders something, and when told they didn't have it, he says 'F**k'. Then the wife turns to him and shouts,

'How many times do I have to tell you not to say fuck in front of the C-H-I-L-D?'

Overheard by PONCHO, Micky D's
Posted on Friday, 16 March 2007

How much is the bus?

A friend of mine had an accident years ago with a chainsaw in which he lost one finger and part of another. We were in a bar one night, about to get a bus to another disco, and a guy shouts

across the bar to him enquiring how much the bus would cost. He put up his hands to signify €10 and the guy shouts back at him, 'What, €8.50?!'

Overheard by Anonymous, pub
Posted on Friday, 16 March 2007

Rough justice

In court a few years back the usual traffic violations were being called up. A man wearing a Dublin Bus uniform and carrying a Dublin Bus bag gets called. The judge asks the prosecuting Garda what he has him here for. 'Driving in a bus lane, your honour,' explains the Garda.

After the courtroom stops laughing the judge says to him, 'You should know better than most as you're a bus driver.'

The accused replies, 'I'm sorry, your honour, but I taut I was in me bus.'

Overheard by Phil, the Four Courts
Posted on Thursday, 15 March 2007

Bono speaks

At the U2 concert in Croke Park, Bono asks the audience for some quiet. Then in the silence, he starts to slowly clap his hands. Holding the audience in total silence, he says into the microphone, 'Every time I clap my hands, a child in Africa dies.'

A voice from near the front of the audience pierces the silence:

'Fookin' stop doin' it, then!'

Overheard by Anonymous, Croke Park, 2005
Posted on Wednesday, 14 March 2007

Sex education gone wrong

While travelling home on the Luas recently, I heard a group of four young girls speak about a class they had that day in school. One announces to the group,

'Oh my God, that was terrifying wasn't it? Who do you think has one, I'd say it's you Amanda, like you were with your man and everyone knows he's been with everyone.'

Amanda: 'The cheek of you, it's not me. Ya heard what Miss said, one in four of your age group have an STI. It could be anyone.'

I think they may have needed less sex education and more Mathematics!

Overheard by Anonymous, on the Luas
Posted on Tuesday, 13 March 2007

8 December

Getting on to a bus on O'Connell Street one day, and there were a few other people getting on. Just before it was my turn, the guy before me shouted, '1.20 please' to the driver, in a country accent. The bus driver nodded with his head towards the box where you throw the money in. The young lad from the country then leaned over and shouted into the box, '1.20 please!'

Overheard by Anonymous, O'Connell Street
Posted on Tuesday, 13 March 2007

The trouble with neighbours

My cranky no-kids neighbour had a major problem with us unruly brats when we were young (I'm the youngest of seven). After years of listening to her complaints, my older brother had had enough. Calling one day to complain about the family dog she says to my brother, 'My husband is going mad, your dog is always chasing him in the car,' to which my brother replies,

'I'm sorry, Mrs Quinn, my dog doesn't have a car.'

Overheard by Anonymous, at home on the doorstep
Posted on Saturday, 10 March 2007

At the cleaners

Waiting for my turn in a dry-cleaners recently, a man was having difficulty in getting his suit back.

'It's a Giorgio Armani,' said the customer patiently.

'A wha'?' said the assistant.

'A Giorgio Armani!' he replied rather haughtily.

'Hey, Monica, can you find a George O'Malley suit down there?'

Overheard by Anonymous, south Dublin dry-cleaners
Posted on Wednesday, 7 March 2007

Horse on bus

Got on the no. 27 bus into town one morning, and the bus driver was in such a state of convulsive laughter at something he was hearing over the bus radio that he couldn't take my fare. When he eventually calmed down he said,

'There's a horse after getting on the bus in Darndale and they can't get him off!'

Overheard by Anonymous, on the no. 27 bus
Posted on Tuesday, 6 March 2007

One is not amused

On the bus, couldn't help overhearing two old dears …

Old Dear #1: 'So have ya the place ready for the christening?'

Old Dear #2: 'I have. I was scrubbing all week. It's fit for the Queen now.'

Old Dear #1: 'I hear she's a fussy bitch alright.'

Overheard by Cabra Joe, on the no. 121 bus into town
Posted on Monday, 5 March 2007

Haircut?

Girl: 'Hey, how are you? Did you get a haircut?'

Boy: 'What? Are you serious!? Of course I did!'

Girl: 'Jeez, calm down, I wasn't sure.'

Boy: 'What do you mean you're not sure!? I used to have an afro!'

Overheard by Anonymous, Grafton Street
Posted on Saturday, 3 March 2007

Lunatic!

A crowd of us outside Café en Seine on Dawson Street on Saturday night, watching the lunar eclipse, when I overheard a D4 girl answering her mobile phone and exclaiming excitedly,

'Hi Nicola! We're outside watching the moon orbit the sun!'

Nobody bothered correcting her!

Overheard by Pete, Café en Seine on Dawson Street
Posted on Monday, 5 March 2007

Who knew Dublin Bus drivers had chauffeur training?

On the bus home from work before Christmas, absolutely lashing rain. The bus pulls up at a stop, obviously a few feet from the footpath. Doors open but no one gets on, then I hear a roar from outside,

'Can ya move da bus in closer, I'm wearin' sandals!'

… and the driver did!

Overheard by Ali, on the no. 65B bus
Posted on Tuesday, 6 March 2007

Save the moles!

I was in Dublin Airport and I was buying a pack of notebooks for my daughter. They were really thin and bound in cardboard, but it said 'moleskin', so up at the till the lady said, 'Dat'll be €17 there now, love, dat's very spensive isn't it?'

'I know … it's because they are moleskin,' I replied.

Then she said under her breath — not even to me, 'Ah, de poo-ur moles!'

Overheard by Lorcan, Dublin Airport
Posted on Wednesday, 7 March 2007

Fraddles

A friend of my Dad's was going on holiday and wanted to buy some clip-on sunglasses to attach to his specs. He went into a chemist and asked the girl behind the counter if they sold any.

'Fraddles?' asked the shop assistant.

'Yeah, Fraddles, is that what they're called? I'll have a pair of Fraddles, please.'

'No,' said the shop assistant, 'Do you want them FOR ADULTS or children?!'

Overheard by Anonymous, in an unnamed Dublin chemist
Posted on Wednesday, 21 March 2007

Child running for bus

As I am a bus driver for many years with Dublin Bus, I come across some very funny incidents. A woman with two small children was running for the no. 3 bus at Westland Row, so I waited for them. The youngest of the small kids was called (I can only guess) Chantelle. As the mother was calling the child to hurry up, she mouthed,

'Chanfuckintelle, will you hurry up!'

I'm still laughing about it ten years on.

Overheard by Dave, on the no. 3 bus at Westland Row
Posted on Thursday, 8 March 2007

Taxing the lion ...

On O'Connell Street, a charity worker had stopped a pedestrian.

Charity worker: 'Would you like to buy a line, sir?'

Guy: 'I'm from the country, why would I want to buy a lion, sure he'd eat all the sheep ...'

Overheard by Michael, O'Connell Street
Posted on Thursday, 8 March 2007

Happy talk

This is probably one of those 'ya had to be there' things but it still makes me laugh.

Happened about seven years ago, was working in a hotel in the city centre as night manager. I had a night porter on with me who was a lovely fella but had a dreadful stammer. I ordered a taxi for some people leaving a function and this taxi driver comes in and roars, 'Did y-y-youse order a Teh-teh-teh-TAXI?'

With that the night porter appears from the back office with this big, angry head on him and says,

'Are you tay-tay-tay-takin' de p-p-p-piss owra m-m-m-me?'

Overheard by Snow White, hotel in city centre
Posted on Friday, 9 March 2007

Tony O'Toole's fault!

While waiting for my luggage at carousel no. 3 at Dublin Airport, a voice over the intercom:

'Whoever's waiting at carousel no. 3, move to no. 5, 'cos Tony O'Toole broke it!'

Overheard by Anonymous, baggage at Dublin Airport
Posted on Wednesday, 7 March 2007

Safe as houses

My slightly superior neighbour was boasting to my Mam about how fantastic her precious youngest son was doing since emigrating to New York. She said, 'Oh he's doing brilliant, he's living in one of the condoms that they're all living in over there.'

My mother just smiled smugly.

Maybe I'm out of touch but I think she meant condominium …

Overheard by my Mam, Finglas
Posted on Monday, 5 March 2007

Kids can sometimes be too honest!

I used to work in a well-known 5-star D4 hotel. I took a fancy to their lovely china cups with the hotel's initials printed on them. I didn't think a couple would be missed.

One day I treated my Mam and eight-year-old sister to afternoon tea there. As my colleague served them, my little sister says in a loud voice to my Mam,

'Hey Mam, they have the same cups as us!'

Overheard by Anonymous, D4 hotel
Posted on Saturday, 3 March 2007

I hit a Pole

Last week I was walking in Sandyford near the Mint. A woman driver had her car parked on the path with the hazard lights on. Coming closer it was clear that she had hit a Yield sign when going through a left slip road. She was on the phone telling someone about her accident.

'I hit a pole, luckily there's not much damage to the car …'

'No! A Yield sign, not a Polish person!'

Overheard by Southsider, Sandyford
Posted on Thursday, 1 March 2007

Bring on the harassment lawsuit ...

Coming up to the counter in McDonald's, I heard the middle-aged manager say to the tired-looking girl sweeping the floor, 'Go on, sweep me off my feet.'

I had to bite my lip …

Overheard by Anonymous, McDonald's, Blackrock
Posted on Monday, 26 February 2007

Huh?

Standing waiting with five others for the no. 18 bus in Rathmines. A guy walks by, recognises a familiar face amongst the group and says,

'Ah there yeh are again, Charlie. I saw yeh the other day on O'Connell Street, but by the time I caught up with yeh, you were gone.'

Overheard by Seamus, Rathmines
Posted on Sunday, 25 February 2007

Inspiration for the day

After a long slog all the way from Tallafornia into town on the no. 65 bus, the bus driver pulled up on Dame Street where the majority of people got out, and the bus driver yelled at everybody, 'Fly my pretties, FLY!'

Overheard by Twister, on the no. 65 bus
Posted on Thursday, 22 February 2007

Always in the last place you look

On the no. 111 bus (single decker), we were travelling along behind a no. 7 bus (double decker). They both follow the exact route for 20 minutes or so.

Both buses were pulling up towards a bus stop. The no. 7 lets people off and a fairly scum-baggish looking chap is one of them. He goes to his jeans pocket and it seems like he has lost something.

In the meantime he hasn't noticed the no. 7 leave and the no. 111 pull into the stop to let people off.

He pushes through the people getting off, has a sudden realisation halfway down the bus and says,

'What happened to the f**kin' stairs?'

Overheard by Anonymous, on the no. 111 bus
Posted on Thursday, 22 February 2007

Law abidin'

On a train from Dublin to Galway, August 2006. One very drunk man was causing no end of trouble, to the extent that the train had to be stopped so he could be thrown off. His very embarrassed friend was trying to calm him down, so Mr Drunk roars at him, in a very strong Dub-el-in accent,

'Wha' are yous getting law abidin' on me for? I'll law abide you in a min-a!'

If only …

Overheard by Sweary, train, Dublin to Galway
Posted on Wednesday, 21 February 2007

All 'Fore' Americans

Coming into Dublin, cabin crew distribute cards to non-EU passengers, which for many provides some good entertainment. On one such occasion an American lady proclaimed, 'Excuse me, Mam, this card is looking for four names and I've only got three.'

Rather than getting into the technicalities of the word 'forename', I smiled and told her three names would do nicely.

Overheard by Karen, Aer Lingus flight
Posted on Wednesday, 21 February 2007

Young at heart

Not so much heard as seen.

Was standing in a queue for a bank machine on O'Connell Street beside one of the Londis shops when out bursts this young lad, with a security guard chasing after him. The guard catches up with him and pins him on the ground, and the young lad throws away about six dirty mags that he had stolen.

The security guard proceeds to beat him and this old man on a walking stick walks over and picks up the mags, like he's helping the security guard. Then he abandons his walking stick and runs down the road with one leg trailing behind him.

Some smart-arse shouts after him, 'Run, Forrest, run!' leaving myself in hysterics and a much bemused Asian tourist!

Overheard by Anonymous, O'Connell Street
Posted on Friday, 2 February 2007

Spit

Was in Ballyfermot a few years ago and was waiting to cross at the traffic lights. A young mother was standing beside me and was holding her young son's hand. The boy spat into the pedestrian crossing button, looked up at his mother and exclaimed, 'Mah! Sumwuns goin' teh press dah!'

Overheard by James, traffic lights near Ballyfermot church
Posted on Thursday, 1 February 2007

Late-night Luas

Whilst standing on a late-night Luas to Tallaght, a drunken couple were having a row. The husband, who was crippled, seemed unfazed at the distress he was causing the other passengers. At St James's Hospital, another drunken man stepped on and began accosting the drunken husband for the way he was treating his wife. A verbal row ensued between the drunken trio.

The husband, clearly frustrated, claimed he was going to beat the man up and suggested they should take it outside at the next stop. At this point the wife leans in and whispers some words of advice that nobody in the carriage can hear. The husband responds,

'What do you mean I'm in a f**king wheelchair!?'

Overheard by Kevin, on the bleedin' Daniel Day
Posted on Wednesday, 31 January 2007

Early planning

26 January in Milosky's Woodworkers supply centre in Terenure. One of the staff was making some polite conversation with my father:

'You know, it's only 11 months until St Stephen's Day!'

Overheard by Leo, Milosky's in Terenure
Posted on Tuesday, 30 January 2007

Too much information

After asking the young assistant at the ice-cream stand in the Omni Centre for two ice-cream cones, she says, 'I'll be back in a minute, love, right?'

A lifetime later she comes back, hands me the

ice-creams and says, 'Sorrrreee bout dat, luv, I had te go to de toilet!'

Lovely!

Overheard by Philip, Omni Centre, Santry
Posted on Saturday, 27 January 2007

Final resting place

Some time ago a friend and I were at a funeral. It was cold and raining. On the way from the burial we pass an open grave: very mucky with water puddled at bottom. My friend looks in and says,

'Wouldn't you die if you had to go in there!'

Overheard by Bubbles, Glasnevin Cemetery
Posted on Friday, 26 January 2007

I don't know where she gets it

Heard on the no. 78A bus:

Woman #1: 'Yer little wan's getting awful big, how old is she now?'

Woman #2: 'Oh, Britney's going on four, oh, and you should hear the f**king language out of her. Tell Anto to f**k off, Britney!'

Britney: 'F**k off!'

Woman #2: 'Jaysus, I don't know where she gets the language outta.'

Overheard by Chuck, on the no. 78A bus
Posted on Friday, 26 January 2007

Ahh, Ma!

In a checkout queue behind mother and son (11+) with earphones in and he pipes up in a really loud voice,

'Ahhh, Ma, did you put this Barry Manilow co-pack-arama shite on my iPod?!?!?'

Overheard by Anonymous, Tesco, Clearwater
Posted on Friday, 26 January 2007

Take-away

Late Saturday in Burger King, O'Connell Street, I overheard a young fella ask for a 'BIG MAC', to which the assistant replies, 'Sorry, but that's a McDonald's burger.'

The young fella replies, 'I know, Bud, don't be long!'

Overheard by Frozenthumbs, Burger King
Posted on Thursday, 25 January 2007

Cup of tea

A guy from the inner city works for my uncle in a trophy shop on Marlborough Street. He was making tea for my uncle and a sales rep who had called in. He brings in the two cups of tea and forgets which cup he had put the sugar in, so he takes a slug out of one of the cups and says to the sales rep, 'Yep, that's yours.'

Overheard by Anand, Marlborough Street
Posted on Thursday, 25 January 2007

Extra vanganza!

On the bus coming home from town the other day, just going past Parkgate Motors. Two girls were sitting behind me. One of them turns to the other and asks, 'What is a vangaza?' The other says, 'Wat, why?' 'Well,' she says, 'that garage's cars have extra vangaza!' The other just goes, 'Don't know?'

I looked at the garage, and in big letters it said,

'Car Extravaganza'!

Overheard by Sam, on the no. 25A bus
Posted on Thursday, 25 January 2007

She was clearly confused!

I was walking along the canal beside Portobello College when a swan began to get out of the

canal. A young girl with her boyfriend notices this and says to him excitedly,

'Oh look, the big duck is gettin' out of the sea!'

Overheard by Lou, canal at Portobello
Posted on Thursday, 25 January 2007

National Development Plan me arse!

Overheard an old man in the Cherry Tree pub criticising the government's newly published National Development Plan in which €184 billion will be invested over the next seven years.

He moans, 'For jaysus sake, how am I gonna benefit from dat! Why don't dey just divide the €184 billion by four million people! Dat way we'd all get €46,000 each!?

How did he work that out in his head?

Overheard by Anonymous, Cherry Tree pub, Walkinstown
Posted on Thursday, 25 January 2007

Carnival time in Gort

Passenger #1: 'Did you see your woman from "Coronation Street" is on tonight, trying to trace her ancestors in Gort?'

Passenger #2: 'She'll have a job, the place is full of bleeding Brazilians.'

Overheard by Paddy, on the no. 19 bus to Rialto
Posted on Wednesday, 24 January 2007

A good catch

In Tamango's niteclub several years ago a guy kept asking my friend up to dance and she kept turning him down. After about an hour of him pestering her, we left the club.

As we were leaving, he turned and shouted, 'I didn't catch your name.'

To which my friend replied, 'I didn't f**king throw it at you!'

Overheard by Amanda, Tamango's at the
White Sands Hotel, Portmarnock
Posted on Wednesday, 24 January 2007

Drunk as a skunk

Drunk girl: 'You are locked!'

Drunk man (practically being carried by the girl): 'I amn't!'

Drunk girl: 'Fifty euro says you wet the bed!'

Overheard by Anonymous, outside the
Foggy Dew on Dame Street
Posted on Tuesday, 23 January 2007

Toilet break

Getting off the no. 16 bus in Terenure, I wonder why the driver is turning off the bus engine. As I'm stepping off the bus, the driver gets out of the driver's cab and I hear him say loudly to all the people on the bus,

'I'm running into the Spar to use the toilet, I'll

be back in a minute, but don't worry I'll get yous all ice-creams!'

I giggled all the way down the road!

Overheard by Clare, Terenure village
Posted on Sunday, 21 January 2007

Kids in pubs, what do you expect?

In the pub over Christmas one afternoon. There's a gang of lads in the corner, and one of them had his son with him. This kid, about four or five, suddenly gets up and grabs his coat.

'Where you going?' his dad asks.

'Out for a smoke,' the little fella answers.

Overheard by AG, Skerries
Posted on Thursday, 18 January 2007

Whiskey in the bar

A friend of mine was in a bar in Malahide and he asked the (Polish) girl behind the counter for a 'Paddy'. She went and filled him a glass of 'Powers'.

He said nothing the first time, but the second time, as she was heading for the 'Powers' again, he said, 'There's a bottle of Paddy on the shelf there.'

'Oh' she said, 'I thought they were the same. Everywhere I go I see "Paddy Powers"!'

Overheard by Stephen, Malahide
Posted on Wednesday, 17 January 2007

Oh dear

At the Zoo during the weekend, I was looking at the penguins, when I overheard a women telling her son, 'Ah, look at the ducks!'

Overheard by Jane, Dublin Zoo
Posted on Wednesday, 17 January 2007

Nick-Nack-Paddy-Wack-in-the-Ilac

In the Ilac Centre on Saturday, waiting at the ground floor for the lift to the car park. A large group of people were also waiting. As the lift doors open, we all wait for the lift to empty before piling on. Standing at the back of the lift that quickly became full, leaving a group of six or seven unable to fit on.

One woman about 50 years old, bloke's haircut, bleach blond/yellow, about 5 foot, typical wife-swap head on her, starts telling everyone to push back so she could fit on. Everyone looks around and sees there is no room. A man at the front tells the woman, 'There is no room.'

She says, 'Push back!'

He says, 'There is no room, just wait.'

Furiously, she says, 'Diya want me to drag ya out of da lift and ya can bleedin' wait?'

Everyone just sniggered at her muppet mentality and the lift doors closed in her face.

Classic.

Overheard by Stephen, Ilac Centre
Posted on Monday, 15 January 2007

Never wear a short skirt ...

I was out on Friday night with a couple of girls I used to work with. One of them, who shall remain nameless to spare her blushes, was wearing high heels and an incredibly short skirt. We were walking from one pub to another when a group of four lads, about fifteen years old, passed us and quick as a flash one pipes up,

'Jaysus, if I'd legs like that I'd walk on me hands!'

Overheard by Anonymous, Wexford Street
Posted on Monday, 15 January 2007

Anybody there?

I was in a pub toilet the other night and an obviously drunk woman stumbled in.

'Mary!' she called.

'Yeah?'

'Are you in here?'

A pause, as 'Mary' thought about this: 'Yeah.'

The rest of the queue was in stitches!

Overheard by Tina, ladies' toilets, Frazers
Posted on Sunday, 14 January 2007

Free green thingies

While shopping in Tesco, my girlfriend's mother is packing her bags while the girl behind the till is scanning her shopping. She picks up one of the items and holding it up says,

'Wha's dat?'

'It's an avocado.'

'Av-a-wha?'

'Avocado.'

'Ah f**k it,' she says and throws it into one of the bags — without scanning it.

Overheard by Anonymous, Tesco, Finglas
Posted on Saturday, 13 January 2007

Monkey magic

On entering Dublin Zoo not so long ago, there was a monkey swinging from his treehouse to a tree via rope and making — well — monkey sounds! Then I overhear a little girl about seven ask her mother, 'Maa, is that monkey real?'

Her bigger brother then interrupts: 'Nooo! It's a bleeding man in a monkey suit, ya thick ya!'

Then the mother clips the lad on the head and says, 'Don't f**king ruin it for her, ya little b*ll*x!'

Ahh, ignorance is bliss!

Overheard by Pips, Dublin Zoo
Posted on Friday, 12 January 2007

I'm on the night train — bottoms up!

The Sunday Waterford-to-Dublin rail service had recently banned alcohol on the service, prohibiting all alcohol on board, in addition to roving security patrols up and down the train. The reason for the Elliot Ness style clamp-down was gregarious hoards of anti-social commuters clambering aboard after a heavy weekend in Kilkenny, still pissed, smoking pot, drinking their voddy and fouling the air with their nasal tones and mangled grammar, not to mention their booze-infused flatus.

To copperfasten Irish Rail's no-nonsense intent, the announcer on the PA announced the following one evening:

'This is the five o'clock service from Plunkett Station Waterford to Heuston Station Dublin. THERE IS NO ALCOHOL PERMITTED ANYWHERE ON THIS TRAIN, there is no baggage permitted on seats, there is no smoking permitted anywhere on this service including toilets. Anybody found contravening this will be removed from the train by the Gardaí at the next station.'

There was a pause and then the mic was keyed again:

'Just stay quiet and you'll get there.'

Overheard by Jack, Waterford to Dublin train
Posted on Friday, 12 January 2007

Talk isn't cheap

Was standing outside the post office on Cork Street, waiting for it to open, when this auld one started chatting to me.

The conversation got around to the ever-increasing house prices. She told me that because it is so expensive to buy in Dublin, her daughter and her daughter's husband had to buy a house in Co. Meath but, 'Dey don't like it

ar all 'cos dey hafta commUUN-icate for two
hours a day.'

Overheard by Danixx, Cork Street
Posted on Friday, 12 January 2007

Bad manners

I was sitting on a bench in Malahide Castle when
a couple with a young girl came and sat on the
bench opposite me. The mother gave the little
girl an orange to keep her quiet.

The parents were in the middle of a
conversation when the child began to sob
loudly. Juice from the orange had squirted into
her face. When asked what was wrong, the little
girl tearfully stated,

'The orange spat at me!'

Overheard by Amy, Malahide Castle
Posted on Friday, 12 January 2007

Can you bring me the bill, please?

I was sitting in a coffee shop having lunch and a
mother and her young daughter were sitting at
the table next to me. On finishing their lunch,
the young girl went into the bathroom.

A few minutes later, obviously having had a bout
of diarrhoea, she came out and announced
loudly to her mother,

'Mommy, Mommy, my poo has melted!'

Overheard by Ann, coffee shop in Malahide
Posted on Friday, 12 January 2007

Chivalry me arse

I was out driving the car along Kevin Street when it broke down. Got out of the car and was looking at it when a young fella passing by shouted,

'Hey missus, do you wanta push?'

I said, 'Yes please.'

He said, 'Go ahead!'

Overheard by Ann, Kevin Street
Posted on Friday, 12 January 2007

Teddy bear's bum

Donegal teacher teaching in a Dublin school. She shows the children a map of Ireland and shows them where Donegal is. She tells them that Ireland is shaped like a teddy bear, so Donegal is the head i.e. the brains of the country.

A week later, Co. Wexford came up in conversation. A child asked where on the teddy bear was Wexford. When they were shown, one wee fella said,

'Ah jaysus, Miss, I wouldn't go there on me holidays!'

Overheard by Anne (I was the teacher), in a Dublin school
Posted on Friday, 12 January 2007

The science of alcohol

In Pravda, Thursday night, outside having a smoke. This couple are on their way inside. She turns around and says to him, 'It's not as cold as it was earlier.'

Guy behind them: 'That's 'cos you're locked.'

Thought it was classic.

Overheard by Big Al, outside Pravda pub
Posted on Friday, 12 January 2007

A youthful imagination

On the bus last Thursday and this mother gets on with her four-year-old daughter. The daughter sits down first and then the mother beside her. Immediately the child starts crying.

When her mother asks her what the problem is, she replies, tearfully, 'You sat on Jalu!'

I can only assume 'Jalu' was an imaginary friend …

Overheard by Sean, on the no. 16 bus, Rathfarnham
Posted on Thursday, 11 January 2007

Nothing in life is free, not even the Herald!

Walking past the start of the Luas line at St Stephen's Green. A man is selling the *Evening Herald*. A young woman walks past and takes a newspaper from him. She then proceeds to walk away. He looks at her, puzzled and says, 'Eh, one euro please.'

She hands it back to him: 'Sorry I thought it was free.'

Overheard by Ciara-Ann, outside St Stephen's Green
at the Luas stop
Posted on Thursday, 11 January 2007

Inflation nation

A New York friend of mine was in Dublin over the Christmas and New Year period. He had finally got to grips with Dublin's confusing transport system and had even got the hang of the exact change fare on the buses (having been stung with getting no change on more than one occasion).

On New Year's Day he got on a bus with his exact change, only to discover the fare had gone up by 5c. He says to the driver,

'Geez man, it was €1.35 yesterday, what the hell is goin' on?'

To which the driver replies, dead pan, 'Happy New Year!'

Overheard by Anna, on Dublin bus
Posted on Thursday, 11 January 2007

Do It Yourself

I used to work in a B&Q hardware store. A woman walked in one day and I overheard her ask,

'Do you know anywhere around here where I can get nailed?'

Overheard by Miley, B&Q, Airside Retail Park, Swords
Posted on Thursday, 11 January 2007

Painful passing experience

In the local pub one evening, decided to use the toilets (once the seal is broken, have to go every half hour).

Picture the scene: three urinals and the one in the middle is the only one free. I tend to suffer from stage fright and the fact that two guys were standing on either side of me didn't help matters. The guy on my left said,

'Jaysus, I'll have to pay a visit to the doctor, this is now beyond a joke.'

I asked was everything ok, to which came the reply,

'I don't think so ... I keep pissing these Blue Lumps.' (Channel Blocks)

Needless to say, I almost wet myself!

Overheard by Keith, Tolka House
Posted on Wednesday, 10 January 2007

Real Dublin poetry

At the Dublin versus Mayo match last autumn, a mate of mine on the Cusack Stand overheard another supporter say,

'Ah jaysus, dere's a great sight … the hill wavin' like a showal a' mackerill!'

A truly beautiful simile!

Overheard by Rob, Croke Park
Posted on Wednesday, 10 January 2007

Sarky security

Standing in Arnotts a few weeks back, I overheard some 'chung wan' ask the security man where the bargain basement was.

He was on the ball and replied, 'First floor.'

Overheard by Biffo, Arnotts
Posted on Wednesday, 10 January 2007

A hard pill to swallow

Years ago, a group of us, while returning from college on the DART, were yapping away as students are wont to do. One member of the group was going on a bit much about some academic nonsense — in fact we had all tuned out with boredom — when an auld fella on the seat beside us turned to him and said,

'Hav yez got a Disprin or a Anadin?'

We shrugged and the auld fella pointed at our boring friend and said,

'Cos I have a pain in me b*llix listenin' to tha'
shite!'

Overheard by Rob, on the DART
Posted on Wednesday, 10 January 2007

All you need is love

Waiting for the train yesterday at Pearse Station,
when I overheard a girl beside me (a real
Howaya) trying to get her boyfriend to stop
grabbing her.

Or, as she put it, 'Stop feelin' me bleeedin'
hole!'

Overheard by Count Dooku, Pearse Station
Posted on Wednesday, 10 January 2007

Terminology crisis

In a training class today in the office, the trainer
apologised in advance, explaining that the
course material was new and that we were the
first class she was going to train on it, so we
would be her …

Before she could say it, the loo-la Spanish bird
in the office that has not been able to manage
English pronunciation despite four years in
Dublin, shouts out …

'We will be Guinness Pigs!'

Priceless, never a truer word said, I pondered.

Overheard by Swissoff, in the office
Posted on Wednesday, 10 January 2007

Lift of sardines ... and one tomato

In a lift at Arnotts in town a few weeks ago. Quite squashed. The lift stops on the first floor and this couple are waiting to get in, but nobody gets out. This guy gets in and says, 'Ah, come on, Mary, there's enough room here, these people will shift!'

When she still shows reluctance, and obvious embarrassment, some guy shouts from the back, 'C'mon, Mary!'

Soon everyone's saying, 'C'mon, Mary!'

She gets on with a face like a tomato!

Overheard by Sean, Arnotts in town
Posted on Tuesday, 9 January 2007

Olden days

I was walking through town the other day and an old gent in front of me tripped and fell. Naturally, I helped him up, and in doing so he said,

'Jaysus, they don't make paths like they use to, that wouldn't have happened in my day, damn foreigners.'

Of course, I agreed with the aul' racist!

Overheard by Mike, city centre
Posted on Tuesday, 9 January 2007

He ain't heavy ...

Guy#1: 'How's that brother of yours?'
Guy#2: 'He is still a miserable f**ker.'

Guy#1: 'Ah c'mon, he's not dat bad.'

Guy#2: 'I only talk to him in case I need a transplant, or bone marrow.'

Overheard by P, McDonald's, Dublin Airport
Posted on Tuesday, 9 January 2007

He actually had to think about that

Hanging around the old Dundrum Shopping Centre last Sunday, I overheard these guys talking:

Guy#1: 'Yeah, I had salmonella dere a few years ago.'

Guy#2: 'Did yeh die?'

Silence for a few seconds.

Guy#1: 'Nope.'

Overheard by Sean, the old Dundrum Shopping Centre
Posted on Monday, 8 January 2007

The sandwich maker

In O'Brien's Sandwich bar the other day and the girl who was about to make my sandwich turns to her work mate and says,

'I f**kin' hate makin' sandwiches.'

Overheard by Janine, O'Brien's, Blanchardstown
Posted on Monday, 8 January 2007

The common language

Bus from Phoenix Park to town, heading up the quays. Two Dublin girls sitting behind me.

Dublin Girl: 'Why do all deese forddinerts come over heeor?'

To which her friend replied, 'Dey learn de English langwitch.'

Dublin Girl: 'Why do dey wan teh learn deh English langwitch?'

Response: 'Cos it's deh most comminist langwitch in da world.'

With that, the younger of the two young women responds, at the top of her voice for the whole bus to hear (you know the type) …

'I speak English and I don't go arowind braginn dah im BALEEEDIN' COMMIN!'

The looks she got from tourists was priceless and of course, the rest of us Irish on the bus were nearly in tears.

Overheard by Magillycuddyreeks, bus from Phoenix Park
Posted on Monday, 8 January 2007

D4

This was in a lecture in UCD and the lecturer was trying to determine how many D4 heads were in the class (for some reason).

Lecturer: 'So, hands up who thinks they might be considered a D4 type.'

No response until after five minutes of silence.

Some student: 'Well, it's not very D4 to say you're a D4.'

Overheard by Stephen, lecture in UCD
Posted on Sunday, 7 January 2007

Mistaken identity

A few weeks ago walking past the statue of Phil Lynott I noticed an American couple. The wife (I presume) said,

'Quick, George, take a photo of me beside Michael Jackson!'

Overheard by Higgs, Grafton Street
Posted on Friday, 5 January 2007

Late buses

Several years ago, I was on the no. 123 Imp bus in Dublin. It was a dark and rainy day and the traffic was mad. The buses were all running late. The crowded bus I was on stopped at Eason's on O'Connell Street to let two people off and two on, when a distraught lady soaking wet at the bus stop said to the driver,

'This is a disgrace, you're really late, I've been waiting here for ages in the rain, there's supposed to be a bus here every 20 minutes,' to which the driver replied,

'Every eight minutes, luv!' closed the door — and drove on.

Overheard by DuffMan, no. 123 bus
Posted on Friday, 5 January 2007

Plastic bag required at back of bus

Recently while taking the no. 16 bus home I had one of the funniest encounters with a Dublin Drunk.

I was sitting upstairs on the back seat with a friend. At one of the stops the drunk got on, and managed to get up the stairs and stumble down to the back seat. The bus was jammers as usual and the only seats left available were the two between me and the drunk.

A couple of minutes later he suddenly turned to me and asked for a plastic bag. Which I didn't have. He turned back around to face the corner of the bus and started urinating.

Well, I've never seen the top of a bus empty so fast, and to this day I've been wondering would a plastic bag really have helped.

Overheard by Paul, on the no. 16 bus
Posted on Friday, 5 January 2007

Doggie bag optional

A friend of mine lives in an exclusive gated compound in Foxrock — from the outside it looks like one huge enormous mansion.

One night she took a taxi home. Upon approaching the security gate and surveying the 'estate', the taxi driver appraised the swanky property as follows:

'Shur this is the dog's b*llix!'

Overheard by VooDoo, Foxrock dinner party
Posted on Friday, 5 January 2007

Discover Ireland

While on a bus trip from Galway to Dublin, a group of friends were sitting behind me.

Girl: 'Sorry, driver, where are we now?'

Driver: 'Moate.'(Westmeath)

Girl (to her friends): 'We're in Howth, lads, deadly, sure we're nearly home.'

Overheard by Anonymous, bus from Galway to Dublin
Posted on Thursday, 4 January 2007

In times of crisis listen to your stomach

I was on a rugby tour to Milan a couple years ago and as the plane took off from Dublin, an Italian man up the front got into difficulty. There was a big commotion and the stewards laid him on the floor. After a minute the pilot came on and announced the man was having heart trouble and that we were returning to Dublin to get him to a hospital. Then, as the guy lies there, one of the old boys travelling with the team (who had been in the airport bar prior to departure) shouts out,

'If he DIES, can I have his BREAKFAST?!'

Practically the whole plane broke into highly inappropriate laughter. I don't think any Italians got it though.

Overheard by Garrett, Aer Lingus flight EI737 to Milan

Posted on Thursday, 4 January 2007

The ice-cream house

Standing outside Áras an Uachtarain and a woman is standing beside us with her child. The little girl asks, 'Mammy, what's the name of that house?'

The mother informs her child that the name of the house is 'Áras an uactar reoite' (the ice-cream house)!

Overheard by Niamh, in the Phoenix Park
outside Áras an Uachtarain

Posted on Tuesday, 2 January 2007

Boxing Day

Many moons ago one St Stephen's night I was walking down Swords Main Street and overheard two teenage girls discussing the Christmas TV.

'Did ye see "Michael Collins" last night?' enquired one.

The other, with completely the wrong end of the stick, replies, 'No, me Ma HATES boxing!'

Overheard by Hugh, Main Street, Swords

Posted on Tuesday, 2 January 2007

You couldn't make it up

Old couple queuing for the last bus on Abbey Street, 11.30, 1 January:

Woman: 'Very cold, isn't it?'

Man: 'Yes, I'd say it's the coldest night this year.'

Overheard by Bren, queuing for last bus on 1 January
Posted on Saturday, 2 January 2007

Buy drinks but you can't smoke

Was at Centra of Stoneybatter during the Christmas holidays, where two kids not more than seventeen years old were buying two bottles of Jack Daniels and two six-packs of beer. Once they paid for all the drinks, one of the kids returns to the cash point and asks for 20 Silk Cut Purple. The reply of the cashier was, 'You are too young to buy cigarettes.'

Old enough to drink, but not old enough to smoke?

Overheard by C&P, Centra in Stoneybatter
Posted on Tuesday, 2 January 2007

It's a clean machine

A few years ago, a woman, recently returned from Germany where they like things neat and pristine, boarded a no. 7 bus. Looking around the bus, she saw the discarded tickets and other litter on the floor. She turned to the bus driver and said, 'This bus is filthy.'

To which he replied without a moment's

hesitation, 'Well, get off and wait for a clean one then.'

Overheard by Anonymous, on the no. 7 bus
Posted on Monday, 1 January 2007

Dubliners' sympathy for the Yanks

Sitting in a bar in town listening to an Irish trad band with a group of American tourists. They were all really into the music and everything was nice and relaxed. After a while a young Dublin couple sat down very close to a few of the Yanks and struck up a conversation.

Dublin couple: 'So how do ye like it here?'

Yanks: 'Yes, very enjoyable.'

Dublin couple (man): 'September 11th must have been pretty shite?'

Yanks: 'Oh yes ...' interrupted by Dublin couple (woman):

'Forget that, what about the Smoking Ban ...'

Overheard by Lucy, pub in Dublin city
Posted on Friday, 29 December 2006

Ah bless

I was on the no. 17A bus last week when an old man and his grandson got on. We were stuck in traffic outside a school. The little boy looked out the window and saw three girls that looked very similar, so he shouts out,

'Grandda, are they three little twins?'

Overheard by Pauline, on the no. 17A bus
Posted on Friday, 29 December 2006

Losing weight in Finglas

Two women were chatting on leaving the local community centre after attending a weight-loss meeting.

'I don't like that instructor,' said the first woman.

'Why?' replied her friend.

'I prefer the one we had last week — she weighs you lighter!'

Overheard by Emer, outside a weight-loss meeting in Finglas
Posted on Friday, 29 December 2006

The photographer

I was on the no. 39 bus the other night, and overheard three girls, one of whom had a camera. There was a bit of a discussion as to who would take a photo.

One said to the others, 'Look, I'll take the bleedin' photo, after all I AM the photographicis!'

Overheard by Paddy, on the no. 39
bus coming from Blanchardstown
Posted on Friday, 29 December 2006

BLT without the LT please

I was in a sandwich shop in town recently. There's a guy ahead of me in the queue — didn't look like the sharpest knife in the drawer — anyway, he proceeds to order a BLT baguette.

However, he wanted it 'without lettuce or tomato' …

Overheard by Tav, sandwich shop
Posted on Friday, 29 December 2006

Holy God!

Sitting in a church on the northside of Dublin last Christmas Eve. It was the children's Christmas mass, so full of excited kiddies. We were early so were waiting for the mass to begin and one little girl in front kept asking her Dad, 'Daddy, where's Holy God?' to which he replied, 'He'll be out in a few minutes.'

She repeated the question numerous times, while the father was getting less and less patient with her. Eventually she said, one last time,

'Daddy, where's Holy God?' to which he replied loudly,

'HE'S AWAY IN A MANGER!'

The first three rows of the church were in fits!

Overheard by Fiona, Lisa & Jamie, St Canice's Church
Posted on Tuesday, 12 December 2006

Greetings

Was strolling down O'Connell Street when three teenage skanger birds were walking by me. One of their mobiles goes off. It was obviously one of her friends and she answered affectionately, 'Howareya slu'?'

Overheard by Anonymous, O'Connell Street
Posted on Friday, 29 December 2006

The great escape

My aunt and uncle are quite strict on their children. One of the rules was that the front garden gate must not, under any circumstances, be open in case their four-year-old son got out.

I was babysitting him one day and he rushed into the room where I was watching TV, a look of sheer horror on his face:

'Patrick, come quick! The gate is open and I might get out!'

Overheard by Froosh, uncle's house
Posted on Tuesday, 26 December 2006

An ecumenical matter

While waiting in A&E in St Vincent's Hospital, people naturally have to give some personal details. I overheard a girl replying to the question 'What religion are you?' with 'Normal'!

Overheard by Anonymous, A&E department, St Vincent's Hospital
Posted on Friday, 29 December 2006

What a return!

During the summer, while Bushy Park skate park was still under construction (right beside the tennis courts), some skateboarders were kicked off the site and decided to play tennis. One of the boys was using his board as a racket.

An old posh woman who was playing with her husband/partner a few courts away came over and said, 'I don't like the way you're playing tennis with that skateboard.'

Skateboarder quickly and wittily replied,

'Well, I don't like the way you're playing tennis with tha racket!'

Overheard by Brian, Bushy Park
Posted on Tuesday, 26 December 2006

Austin Powers for kids

A couple of years ago, when *Austin Powers* first came out on DVD, I was working in Chartbusters (Phibsboro). One evening I was out on the floor tidying up the DVD display. A concerned woman came up to me with a copy of *Austin Powers*. Pointing to the age certificate, which happened to be 15s, she asked,

'Excuse me, do you have this in 12s?'

Overheard by Ciarán, Chartbusters, Phibsboro
Posted on Monday, 25 December 2006

Last chance

Best ever flight I was on was with Go Airlines a few years back. Just before take-off the air hostess was getting ready for her safety routine, when the pilot came over the mic saying,

'Ladies and gentlemen, please pay attention to the safety instructions as this may be the last chance you ever get ...'

Overheard by Eileen, Go Airlines, Dublin Airport
Posted on Friday, 22 December 2006

Cosmic Lady

Was on the Nitelink home from town last night and a woman who looked a bit crazy turned around to me and asked, 'Excuse me, do you have today's date?'

'It's the 21st of December,' I said, 'shortest day of the year.'

'Oh yes,' she replied, 'The world splits into two today doesn't it.'

What could I say to that?!

Overheard by Podge, Nitelink
Posted on Friday, 22 December 2006

Money

In the barber's the other day the barber was trying to make conversation with a young lad of about thirteen or fourteen.

Barber: 'Are you getting anything for Christmas?'

Young Lad: 'Money.'

Cue a few laughs from the people under their breath who were waiting.

Barber: 'Is that it?'

Young Lad: 'Yeah, I wouldn't trust me Ma to buy anything for me!'

Cue more laughs.

Overheard by Paul, Shaves, Balbriggan
Posted on Friday, 22 December 2006

El radio

My auntie was over in the Canaries and brought a load of stuff back for the family. She bought my Gran a small stereo for her kitchen. My Gran said she couldn't possibly have it in the house.

'Why not?' says my auntie.

'I'll buy one here … all this thing will do is play Spanish radio stations, and I like listening to Gerry Ryan in the morning!'

Overheard by Simon, family home
Posted on Friday, 22 December 2006

Birdman of Finglas

I was in the local day care centre, collecting my mother-in-law, when I noticed a man holding a Zimmer frame, slowly walking past the room I was in. He stops at the door and shouts, 'CUCKOOOOOO', then waddles off, breaking his shite laughing all the way down the corridor!

Overheard by Philip, day care centre, Finglas West
Posted on Thursday, 21 December 2006

Little cutie

Mother wheeling pram with cute one-year-old boy in Smithfield. Along comes her friend Mary (she hasn't seen her for some time):

Mother: 'Howya, Mary, this is little Paddy.'

Mary: 'Jazsus, he's a lovely little b*ll*x.'

Overheard by Brian, Smithfield
Posted on Thursday, 21 December 2006

Flying without brains

Two D4 girls at Dublin Airport, going through security. One girl walks through detectors. It beeps and she gets all afraid.

Security: 'Remove your boots, please.'

D4 girl #1: 'Oh, sorry.'

She walks through again with the BOOTS IN HER HAND! She seems surprised when it beeps again! DOPE!

D4 girl #2 goes through fine.

Security: 'Have you any fluids in your bag?'

D4 girl #2: 'No … just water.'

Overheard by Eadz nd Natz, Dublin Airport
Posted on Wednesday, 20 December 2006

Carol singers slacking off!

I was walking up Grafton Street, past some carol singers taking a rest from singing on a cold night. Two lads walked past me, and one goes to the other in a really disgruntled Dublin accent,

'Jaaaysus, I thought dey were supposed to sing for me money!'

He'd work 'em to the bone!

Overheard by John, Grafton Street
Posted on Wednesday, 20 December 2006

Interior decorating?

Having lunch with the lads while working in Dublin Airport, the conversation turns to the mots.

First Bloke: 'So how's the new mot, what's she like?'

Second Bloke: 'Ah jaysus yeah, she's lovely, has red hair!'

First Bloke: 'Really, and does the carpet match the curtains?'

Second Bloke: 'I don't bleedin' know, I was never in her gaff!'

Overheard by G, lunchtime at Dublin Airport
Posted on Tuesday, 19 December 2006

I wonder if he passed?!

I was walking past the Driving Test Centre in Finglas. There was a Dublin Bus trainee and his tester walking side by side, towards the red learner bus, obviously to do his test. I overheard the trainee saying to the tester,

'Did ya ever drive a bus yerself, Boss?'

Overheard by Bob, Finglas Test Centre
Posted on Monday, 18 December 2006

Dub uses poetic licence

Had to go to hospital the other night. I was sitting in A&E when this guy who looked like Lorcan from *Fair City* came in, shouting and roaring. The nurse asked what was wrong, and he pointed at his blood-soaked leg and said,

'Hurry up, will yiz, I'm bleeeeeeedin' bleedin'!'

Overheard by Paulie, St Vincent's
Posted on Monday, 18 December 2006

Have you ever ordered a sandwich before?

Standing in the queue for a sandwich in O'Brien's in the Omni Centre:

Customer: 'Can I have a sandwich, please?'

O'Brien's Girl: 'Brown or white?'

Customer: 'What?'

O'Brien's Girl: 'Brown or white bread?'

Customer: 'White.'

O'Brien's Girl: 'Butter or mayo?'

Customer: 'What?'

O'Brien's Girl: 'Butter or mayo?'

Customer: 'Eh, butter.'

O'Brien's Girl: 'What would you like?'

Customer: 'Chicken.'

O'Brien's Girl: 'That all?'

Customer: 'Eh … cheese.'

O'Brien's Girl: 'That it?'

Customer: (silence)

O'Brien's Girl: 'Anything else?'

Customer: 'Lettuce. Oh, and coleslaw.'

O'Brien's Girl: 'Anything to drink?'

Customer: 'Tea.'

O'Brien's Girl: 'Medium or large?'

Customer: 'What?'

And so on. Needless to say, when he got to the counter to pay for it, he couldn't remember what he'd ordered!

Overheard by The Dude, Santry
Posted on Monday, 18 December 2006

A long way from home

League final 2005, Armagh versus Wexford. Was sitting in front of about six fellas from Wexford, having the craic before throw in. There was an announcement over the tannoy:

'Could the parents of a little girl who is lost please make their way to the First Aid room. Her name is Kimberley and she's from New York.'

Quick as lightning, one of the Wexford fellas says,

'New York!? Feck me, she *is* lost!'

Overheard by Lorraine, Croke Park
Posted on Monday, 18 December 2006

The complexity of shopping these days

In Dunnes Stores on Saturday, the girl in front of me at the checkout asks the checkout operator, 'How much are yizzer 30c bags?'

Overheard by Jess, Dunnes Stores, The Square
Posted on Monday, 18 December 2006

What they teach them in school nowadays

While dropping my son to school the other day, we passed by the school's large crib with the nativity scene.

My son pipes up: 'I know about baby Jesus!'

Dad: 'Really? Who was he?'

Son: 'Baby Jesus is a sheep.'

Dad: 'No, he's not!'

Son: 'Yes, he is! He's the Lamb of God!'

There's really no response to that, is there?

Overheard by Shay, at my son's school
Posted on Friday, 15 December 2006

In the bookies

Recently while putting on a bet for a mate, I heard two guys talking and the conversation went like this.

First Guy: 'Well Mick, any luck on the 2:45?'

Second Guy: 'Do you know the expression —

beat on the post by a head?'

First Guy: 'Yeah.'

Second Guy: 'Well my horse was ... beat on the head by a post.'

Needless to say, his horse came nowhere.

Overheard by Keith, betting shop
Posted on Thursday, 14 December 2006

The backwards man

A drunken, old (but jolly) man gets on the bus and sits in the wheelchair-user carer's seat, i.e. facing us all. After a few blasts of banter with a woman and her baby, he loudly asks us all, 'Why are you all sitting backwards anyway?' then continues laughing away to himself ...

Overheard by Podge, on the no. 19 bus on the way to town
Posted on Thursday, 14 December 2006

Mass circumcision

Two oul' fellas discussing the inadequacies of the Luas.

Oul' fella #1: 'They should've linked up the Luas lines.'

Oul' fella #2: 'And the DART.'

Oul' fella #1: 'And have a circle line.'

Oul' fella #2: 'They should have it circumcise the entire city ...'

Overheard by Owen, Connolly Luas stop
Posted on Thursday, 14 December 2006

What a cabbage!

Two lads get on the no. 79 bus on Aston Quay, with McDonald's food. One says to the other as he takes the lettuce out of his burger,

'Jaysus, I hate all this cabbage in me booorgar!'

Overheard by Paul, on the no. 79 bus on the way to Ballyfermot
Posted on Tuesday, 12 December 2006

Laughing in the moonlight

It was late Saturday evening and I was queuing for the AIB pass machine off Grafton Street. I noticed two tourists — a couple — asking a slightly drunk man to take their photo with the Phil Lynott statue. As they posed for the photo they asked him, 'Who is this by the way?' to which he replied,

'Oh, that's Phil Lynott — he was the first black man in Ireland!'

Overheard by Anonymous, Grafton Street
Posted on Monday, 11 December 2006

First time on public transport?

D4 girl getting on the Westport to Dublin bus. She didn't have any change so she said to the driver, 'Can I pay by Laser?'

Overheard by John, on the Westport to Dublin bus
Posted on Sunday, 10 December 2006

Get with it, Santa!

In a hairdresser in Swords last week. There was a woman with her little girl, about four, talking about writing her letter to Santa.

Little girl: 'Can we not just send Santa a text?'

Mam: 'I don't think Santa has a mobile phone.'

Little girl: 'Ah, Mam, sure everyone has a mobile phone these days.'

Overheard by JT, hairdresser in Swords
Posted on Friday, 8 December 2006

Anyone for da mouse?

Christmas time about three or four years ago, myself and a few mates were walking down Henry Street, checking out all the stalls and listening to them shouting out all their Christmas offers: 'Geta ur rapin papor three for a eura,' and so on.

Out of the blue, some auld one with a bread-board that's full of wind-up toy mice for cats on top of an old pram starts to shout, 'Anyone der for da Mouses?'

Didn't know what was funnier — the Mouses, or the fact she was selling them at Christmas. Only in Dublin!

Overheard by Hick, Henry Street
Posted on Friday, 8 December 2006

Mixed doubles

In the local on Sunday afternoon for dinner, the pub was packed with families. There were four lads playing doubles on a pool table. A little girl, about four, runs over to the pool table and starts to mess up their game. There's an almighty screech from the mother:

'Reebbeccaaaa, stop playing with those boys' balls!'

Overheard by Philip, the local
Posted on Thursday, 7 December 2006

Battle of the supermarkets

I was in the South Terrace at a soccer match in Lansdowne Road a few years ago. Niall Quinn had made top goal scorer, and a chant of 'Superquinn, Superquinn, Superquinn!' started. Just as the chant was ending, a man at the back of the crowd shouts,

'Up Tesco!'

The whole crowd burst into laughter.

Overheard by Mick, Lansdowne Road
Posted on Wednesday, 6 December 2006

Ciúnas!

Saw a sign in Image beauty salon in Ballymun:

'Noisy children will be sold as slaves!'

Overheard by Anonymous, Ballymun
Posted on Tuesday, 5 December 2006

Mc Breakfast

While in McDonald's early one morning, a customer asked the cashier, 'What do you have for breakfast?'

To which she replied, 'Ah, usually just a cup of coffee and a slice of toast.'

Customer was not impressed!

Overheard by Anonymous, McDonald's, Donaghmede
Posted on Sunday, 3 December 2006

He knows when you've been bad or good ...

Walking into the Blanchardstown Shopping Centre last week, saw this little kid, about three years old, running in front of me, with his mum and granny pushing a pram behind him.

Little kid twirls around and falls flat on his back. Picks himself up, no bother, but then his Granny breaks into raucous laughter.

'AHAHAHAHAAAA! That's what you get for not holding your Nana's hand. Santy did that to ya!'

Who knew Father Christmas was so vindictive?!

Overheard by TD, Blanchardstown Shopping Centre
Posted on Friday, 1 December 2006

Ah, Dublin logic ...

Two women standing at a bus stop, apparently discussing what to wear on a night out. One says to the other,

'Well, if it's cold, you can always wear those fishnet tights ... you know, the ones with the holes in them.'

Don't ya just love Dublin logic?

Overheard by Ali, at a bus stop on Westmoreland Street
Posted on Tuesday, 28 November 2006

D'yerknowharimean, Bud?

Skanger telling his friend (in a nasal whiney voice) how he fools his ma:

'Sure I smoke away in the front room when me Mudder's ou a bingo. When she comes back I do have me runners off and I'm after rubbin me feet t'geder, so I am, so the smell of me fee covers up the smell of the hash. D'yerknowharimean?'

Overheard by Beatrice, queuing in the chip shop
Posted on Monday, 27 November 2006

Toilet talk

Sitting in the bog in a city-centre pub after a few scoops, the bloke in the next cubicle says, 'Howya, how's it goin'?' to which I reply, 'Ah, not too bad!' Then he says, 'Sorry!' and I say again, 'Not too bad!' Then he says,

'Listen I'll ring you back, there's some lunatic in the jacks next to me!'

I cringed — and waited 'til he left!

Overheard by Peter, Knightsbridge, Bachelors Walk
Posted on Monday, 27 November 2006

New advances in English dictation

Closing time outside a city centre pub. Argy-bargy between a group of my friends and a bunch of skangers; scuffles followed by skangers taking flight. One skanger temporarily detained and pinned to ground by friend. The skanger refutes all and any involvement in said ruckus by screaming … wait for it …

'I didn't do nuthin to no-one never!'

A double double negative!

Overheard by Anonymous, outside city centre pub
Posted on Friday, 24 November 2006

This DART will terminate in …

On the DART between Bray and Greystones, three Loreto Dalkey schoolgirls walk through the carriage. An announcement is made:

'This train will terminate at the next station.'

One of the girls lets out a little yelp, starts flapping her arms, then says loudly,

'Oh my God! Does that mean the train is broken?'

Private school education, eh?

Overheard by Alan, DART from Bray to Greystones
Posted on Thursday, 23 November 2006

Brainbox of the year

In the local boozer after work, and in the corner the *Weakest Link* was on the box.

'What's the capital of Spain?' asks Anne Robinson.

One of the locals shouts out, 'BARCELONA, ye gobshite!'

Overheard by Tony, Bottom of the Hill, Finglas
Posted on Saturday, 18 November 2006

Barbed-wire top

I was recently working at a high-class fundraiser that a good-looking woman with a big pair of breasts and a top with a low cleavage was organising. She was introduced to a new contributor (an old man):

Old Man: 'Can I compliment you on your Barbed-Wire top.'

The woman looked blank …

Old Man continues: 'It protects the property — but doesn't obstruct the view.'

Overheard by Richie, at a fundraiser
Posted on Wednesday, 15 November 2006

The Dublin chipper

Drunk guy goes in to a chipper (real Dublin accent) and approaches the counter where a guy of possibly Indian or middle-eastern descent is working:

Drunk Dub: 'Giz a ray and chips dere.'

Counter guy (in thick foreign accent): 'Flat ray?'

Drunk Dub: 'Ah jaysus no, pump er up a bih for me, will ya!'

Overheard by Abey-baby, chipper near Parkgate Street
Posted on Wednesday, 15 November 2006

Catholic guilt

On Halloween night, I was standing at my bus stop beside three guys who were off to a fancy dress party and were all dressed as priests. When the bus finally came, the three get on and ask how much. The driver tells them 95c each, only to be met with one of the lads replying,

'I remember when Dublin Bus were a friend to the clergy!'

Overheard by Jamie, on the no. 50 bus, Drimnagh
Posted on Tuesday, 14 November 2006

I'm a celebrity, get me outta here!

A few years back, I was having a conversation with a work mate. He began telling me about a party he was at that weekend. He said he arrived and knew everyone there except this one girl. He asked a friend who she was and was told that she was a bit of a smug, snobby bitch who had some claim to fame and was full of herself because of this fact.

He at some opportunity spoke to her during the night, initiating the conversation with, 'Hey, I know you somehow, I recognise your face.'

Apparently the girl began to glow with self obsession until he said,

'Did you …? Did you …? Did you serve me in Boots the other day?'

Needless to say she was disgusted …

Overheard by Stephen, Glasnevin
Posted on Tuesday, 14 November 2006

Fire safety

At work, in our previous offices, we had a sign outside the lifts advising the safety precautions to be taken in using them — fairly normal, except that, under 'In case of fire', some smart-arse had written,

'Bring marshmallows.'

Overheard by Seamus, Booterstown
Posted on Tuesday, 14 November 2006

No speekee Ingrish

Walking along Grafton Street, couple of D4 girls talking about somebody they knew who had adopted a Chinese baby. One of them perplexedly asked,

'Loike, when he grows up, will he think in English?'

Hmmmm …

Overheard by John, Grafton Street
Posted on Tuesday, 14 November 2006

Dreamland …

Sitting at home at the weekend, my girlfriend and my Mam are having a conversation about what's happening at the moment in *Eastenders*.

My Girlfriend: 'She's putting the baby up for adoption.'

My Mam: 'Yeah, it's terrible, the poor child.'

My Dad: 'It's not real life, it's only a television programme.'

My Mam (I love this bit!): 'Ah, get a life!'

Overheard by SB, at home at the weekend
Posted on Monday, 13 November 2006

The northside diet

During the summer I was driving to the airport and stopped at the traffic lights at the back of the Custom House. An Eastern European couple cross the road in front of me, holding hands. The girl was very slim and was dressed in figure-hugging white pants.

I had my window rolled down, and a taxi driver parked in the next lane shouts across in a thick northside accent,

'Jaysus, would ya look at da, all our birds do is stuff their bleedin' faces with burgers and chips!'

Overheard by Paddy, outside the Custom House
Posted on Monday, 13 November 2006

Axe-wielding bus driver

I was on the no. 65 bus to Blessington, and the top deck of the bus had been cordoned off with a bus ticket roll (much like a crime scene). Kids had smashed the upstairs windows.

Upon passing the Jobstown Inn pub, a drunk

proceeded on and stood beside the driver, talking to him through the security screen. Within the first three stops, he had asked the bus driver 101 stupid questions, which the driver was clearly getting angered by.

The drunk then asked the driver, 'What happened upstairs?'

The driver said, 'There was a murder up there earlier.'

The man clearly shocked said, 'What happened?'

The driver then said, 'On the last run there was some drunk asking me stupid questions. So I took me axe out and chopped him up! Now, have ya any more questions?'

The drunk — petrified at this stage — stutters, 'No, next stop's mine thanks.'

Overheard by Gary, on the no. 65 bus
Posted on Sunday, 12 November 2006

Apple tart

A friend of mine ordered a slice of apple tart in the Kylemore café.

'Do ya wanna eat it?' asked the girl behind the counter.

'Pardon?' said my friend.

'I said do ya wanna eat it?' repeated the girl.

'Well, yes,' he said, rather confused.

With that she threw the apple pie in the microwave:

'Ten cent extra.'

Overheard by Exdub, Kylemore café
Posted on Friday, 10 November 2006

Cinders

I was standing outside Burger King on Grafton Street at about four o'clock on a Sunday morning, one shoe in my hand because my feet were killing me.

This lad wearing a white tracksuit comes up to me and asks me can he have my shoe.

'What do ya want my shoe for?' I asked.

'So I can find ya in de mornin!'

Overheard by Ali, Grafton Street
Posted on Friday, 10 November 2006

Guinness is good for you ...

Saw a Guinness truck go down Parnell Street yesterday, with 'EMERGENCY RESPONSE UNIT' written in large letters in the dirt on the back.

Overheard by Anonymous, Parnell Street
Posted on Friday, 10 November 2006

Plan B

At Croke Park. All-Ireland Hurling Final 2006,
Kilkenny versus Cork. Before the end of game,
an announcement comes over the tannoy about
spectators staying off the pitch, and for stewards
to take up their positions.

The game ends. As expected, hundreds of fans
start to run on the pitch to congratulate their
heroes. Over the tannoy, 'Plan B, Plan B, Plan B'.

To add to the hilarity of the moment, 'PLAN B'
was displayed in huge letters on the big screen!

Overheard by the Cat, Croke Park
Posted on Friday, 10 November 2006

Know it all

Worked with a severely irritable and thick French
barman in Temple Bar some time back. Because
of his demeanour he was a constant target for
teasing from the other staff. One afternoon he
could take no more and snapped at us,

'You tink dat I know f**k nothing! I tell you dat
I know f**k all!'

We died …

Overheard by Barman, Temple Bar
Posted on Friday, 10 November 2006

Brothers are great

My daughter was going to her debs. They were
meeting at the Assumption Secondary School in
Walkinstown to get on the coach to the hotel, so

the whole family went down to the school to see her off and have a look at the dresses.

When you walk up the drive, there is a sign saying, 'Slow Pupils Crossing'. Her brother looks at the sign and says,

'I can see why you sent her here!'

Overheard by JDub12, Assumption Secondary School, Walkinstown
Posted on Thursday, 9 November 2006

Supermacs — a family restaurant

Late at night, sitting in Supermacs, I see a large biker guy walk in who is absolutely locked. He proceeds up to the counter and says,

'Gimme a family box — without the father!'

Overheard by Bob, Supermacs
Posted on Thursday, 9 November 2006

Think bigger

A little boy was in the toy shop where I work, begging for a toy. The conversation went like this:

Boy: 'Mom, can I get something small?'

Mom: 'No you can't.'

Boy (thinks for a second): 'Can I get something BIG!?'

Overheard by Brian, toy shop
Posted on Tuesday, 7 November 2006

Throwing her weight around

On the Westport to Dublin train on Sunday after the Ireland versus Australia International Rules disaster. Middle-aged woman with giant (I mean the size of a small country) rear end has just gotten on the train and is bashing into everyone as she attempts to find a seat, then throwing herself around as she tries to get her luggage onto the overhead storage shelf.

With much huffing and puffing, she eventually sits down. A young fella smartly quips,

'Coulda done with you against the Ozzies today, Mrs!'

Overheard by Gerry, Westport to Dublin train
Posted on Monday, 6 November 2006

Aussie does indeed rule

While we were getting hockeyed by Australia in the International Rules match on Sunday, there was an Ozzie woman up on the Hill who kept waving her huge flag whenever her team scored, and the people behind her were getting annoyed since it was in the way.

Then in the 4th quarter when Ireland managed to score one mighty singular point, and she kept her flag down, a voice roared after the clapping,

'Where's your flag now?'

Overheard by Bozboz, Hill 16
Posted on Monday, 6 November 2006

Tight jeans

Me and my sister were walking down Thomas Street when a woman walked by wearing extremely tight jeans. My sister is stunned for a second then just says,

'Jaysus, she must've had to jump off the top of de wardrobe to get into dose ...'

Overheard by Anonymous, Thomas Street
Posted on Sunday, 5 November 2006

Righteous indignation

My mother was doing her weekly shopping in Dunnes. A married couple with their son of about four years of age were selecting a trolley. The small boy told his mother, 'Don't pick that one, Mammy — it's f**ked.'

The mother told the child off for using bad language, only to be told in reply,

'But Daddy SAID it was f**ked.'

Overheard by Seamus, Dunnes Stores, Kilnamanagh
Posted on Saturday, 4 November 2006

Cops and robbers

I had a week off work and was washing my car in my driveway. Two boys, not more than ten years old, were playing cops and robbers on bikes. Everything seemed normal until the 'cop' stopped talking on his imaginary walkie-talkie and informed the robber,

'I don't give a f**k about my job, I'm gonna kick your bleedin' head in.'

Overheard by Seamus, Tallaght
Posted on Saturday, 4 November 2006

Long way to go

On the steps of a church after the funeral of an elderly lady.

One mourner: 'That was very sad.'

Second mourner: 'It was. I'm so depressed I just want to find a nice quiet pub and drink meself into Bolivia.'

Overheard by Anonymous, in Clondalkin
Posted on Saturday, 4 November 2006

Why townies shouldn't do agriculture

Just before the Leaving Cert, I was giving grinds to two D4 girls in Agricultural Science. One of the short questions on the paper was, 'Why would the weather forecast be important to potato farmers in Ireland?'

I would have presumed that everybody who did history in primary school would have learned of the potato famine and blight caused by the unusual muggy weather, but apparently not, as one of the girls replied to me,

'So that farmers will know when to put on sun screen?'

God be with the next generation …

Overheard by K, giving grinds
Posted on Friday, 3 November 2006

World Vision

While walking through Temple Bar with my mother, this guy approached and asked would she like to hear more about 'World Vision'. She replied,

'No tanks, luff, I don't need any glasses.'

She didn't cop on until long after the man had walked by that he wasn't talking about Vision Express ...

Overheard by Rosso, Temple Bar
Posted on Thursday, 2 November 2006

Wise words from a Finglas head

I saw this overweight middle-aged guy out power-walking on Ballygall Road in Finglas. A youngfella from the other side of the road shouts over,

'Hey mister, you'd want to do less of the power eatin!'

Fair play to the big guy, he just laughed and kept booting along.

Overheard by S, Finglas
Posted on Friday, 27 October 2006

That'll learn him

Overheard on Hill 16:

Dublin were all over Roscommon but were failing to hit the target and were running up a high amount of wides. After the tenth or so such wide, some well-mannered educated chap (clearly out of place on Hill 16) pipes up and says,

'Come on, Dublin, let's convert our superiority into scores!'

A reply came from a cider-drinking yobbo,

'Do yiz hear f**king Shakespeare down dere!'

Overheard by Diego, from Hill 16 A5 section
Posted on Wednesday, 25 October 2006

Happy birthday

I was in a pub in town at the weekend, a pretty rowdy pub, when two female guards walked in to verify a reported disturbance. A girl sitting near the door shouts out,

'Whose birthday is it? Get yezer kits off, girls!'

Overheard by Jayo, the International Bar
Posted on Wednesday, 25 October 2006

Edible underwear

The Southern Cross Business Park in Bray. A company called 'The Butlers Pantry' (a food manufacturer) had recently moved in to the estate. The driver of a delivery truck comes over and asks us smokers outside,

'Sorry lads, can you tell me where I can find the Butlers Panties?'

Overheard by Barney, Bray
Posted on Wednesday, 25 October 2006

The cheek!

Walking to work this morning on Dawson Street, spotted a Garda standing beside an illegally-parked van, writing a ticket. Van owner runs out of a local shop and says, 'Is there a problem, Garda?'

Garda: 'Yeah, would you look at that, some eejit is after putting a footpath and double yellow lines under your van — the cheek of them!'

Overheard by Aine, Dawson Street
Posted on Wednesday, 25 October 2006

Feckin' immigrants

I'm Aussie, but lived in Dublin for a few years. Anyway, two weeks or so after I arrived, I got a job, and having walked out of said successful interview at about 2 p.m., thought that I should celebrate with a few jars.

Went into a pub near Aungier Street and ordered a pint. It was almost empty so I started chatting with the barman. A few pints later, he's having one or two himself and we've become new-found best mates. He's going on about how great Australia is, and congratulations on gettin' de job, young lad, and you keep your nose clean now. He even buys me a pint to 'celebrate ye gettin yer start in Dooblin'. Grand.

Then this Polish girl comes in and asks, in fairly broken English, 'Do you hev job I can take, yes?'

He rudely tells her no, and as soon as she leaves, he throws her CV in the bin and says to me, in all seriousness ...

'Feckin' immigrants, comin' here and takin' all our jobs.'

Utter genius!

Overheard by Rory, an unnamed pub
Posted on Saturday, 21 October 2006

BIMBO

Sitting chatting with the gurlies. We were talking about Heather Mills, and one of my friends said, 'Oh yeah, that's the one married to Paul McCartney with the PROSTATE leg!'

Overheard by Wen, straight from a mad mate's mouth!
Posted on Friday, 20 October 2006

Decimalisation

Walking through Phibsboro on the North Circular, a small old woman shouts to a rather large black man, 'I have tha' two shillin's for ya!'

He looks at her confused and shrugs.

'The two shillins — the euro I owe ya!'

Overheard by Gar, Phibsboro
Posted on Friday, 20 October 2006

What's wrong with a knife?

Earlier this year I was working in Habitat. This very southside Dublin girl in her late teens, dressed in designer clothes, walked up to me and asked,

'Do you sell bagel slicers?'

I said I didn't even know such a thing existed and, no, the store never stocked them. She said in all seriousness, as if I had been living in the Dark Ages and the store was some throwback to 50s Ireland,

'Well, like, they have them in *The OC* …' and then turned and walked away.

Television really is warping this generation's minds!

Overheard by Anonymous, at work in Habitat
Posted on Friday, 20 October 2006

Bright spark!

Whilst in Woodie's wandering about, as is a handyman's wont, I came across a salt-of-the-earth Dublin family. They had just passed a stand with solar power lamps on display when the mother got rather excited:

Mother: 'Ah Tom, wouldn't dem lamps be lovel-illy out by de roses in de drive?'

Tom: 'Not bad alright, how much are dey?'

Mother: 'Only €9.99 each.'

Son: 'Ah here, dem solar-powered lamps, I heard 'bout dem, they're a scam.'

Mother: 'Why, what's wrong wit 'em?'

Son: 'Sure dey don't work ... der's no bleedin' sun at night ...'

Overheard by Hick, Woodie's DIY
Posted on Thursday, 19 October 2006

Talking to yourself!

My boyfriend was upstairs on a bus to work one morning. A little girl and her father got on and sat right up the front. The little girl started to talk at the top of her voice, 'Dis is grea, Da, ya can see everythin up here, Ma never lets me si up here!'

The father, looking a bit embarrassed by the daughter's loudness, says, 'Der's no need to shout, I'm sittin righ beside you.'

The little girl replies as loudly as before, 'Righ so, I'll just talk to meself in me own head den.'

Overheard by CS, on a bus to Rathfarnham
Posted on Thursday, 19 October 2006

At the dogs

Many years ago I was at the Dogs in Harold's Cross with my parents — it was my mother's first visit.

Before the fifth race starts, my Ma has a pained expression and says, 'Ah, the poor dog, he must be tired.'

'Which one, Ma?'

'The one with the stripey jacket on, this is his fifth race!'

Overheard by Jinho, at the Dogs, Harold's Cross
Posted on Thursday, 19 October 2006

Just folly me directions

Outside a nightclub on Harcourt Street, I overheard a young fella beside me giving directions to someone how to get there. He says,

'Jaysus, will you just tell the taxi driver it's on "HARD CORE STREET"!'

Bless! These people are the future?

Overheard by Alanjo, Harcourt Street
Posted on Thursday, 19 October 2006

Hot weather, wouldn't you say!

One of those nice hot summer nights, I picked up three girls around the Ringsend area. Nice girls, chatting away on the way to Stephen's Green. In the middle of the conversation one turns to the others and says,

'Jaysus, I'm roasting tonight, this weather is killing me.'

One of the others agrees with her, and to express her feelings on the point replies,

'Yeah, I'm boiling, me knickers are wringing!'

Ahhh, Dub girls — where would you get it!

Overheard by Anonymous, in my taxi in Ringsend
Posted on Thursday, 19 October 2006

Ribena man

Drunk man on the no. 150 bus holding a carton of Ribena turns around to me and says, 'That can't be true, 95% of Irish blackcurrants grow up to be Ribena berries?'

How can you respond to that?

Overheard by Timmy, on the no. 150 bus
Posted on Wednesday, 18 October 2006

Bleedin' embolisms

Coming home from Clonshaugh Industrial Estate the other day, my pal Damo overheard two auld ones talking about multicultural Dublin:

'... Jaysus, there's bleedin' Chinese embolisms everywhere ...'

Trying hard not to picture haemorrhaging on a city-wide scale, he hid his laughter and presumed she meant symbols.

Overheard by Babs, from a pal returning
from Clonshaugh Industrial Estate
Posted on Wednesday, 18 October 2006

Ferocious language

I went to Argos to buy a pocket-sized electronic thesaurus. Upon arriving I located one in the catalogue, filled in the little paper slip with the Argos code and then joined the queue. I handed the paper slip to the cashier who was a middle-aged Dublin lady, and the name of the item popped up on her screen, along with the price.

'So it's an Oxford ... The ... Thes ...
Tyrannosaurus rex at €29.99. Now would you
like to insure him for an extra €3 for three
years?'

I shook my head and said no thanks.

"No, OK, so you don't want to insure him, no
problem love, that's grand, here's your order
number.'

Overheard by Karen, Argos
Posted on Wednesday, 18 October 2006

Friends for less

Working for Vodafone years ago, had a
promotion called Friends For Less, basically
nominate three 087 numbers you ring the most
to save money. Anyway, we'd always ask
customers at the end of the call do they want to
register three numbers. Had some muck savage
on who replied, 'Ya, sure, I'll go for 2, 6 and 8!'

!?!?!?

Overheard by Will, while working at Vodafone
Posted on Monday, 16 October 2006

Preparing for an evening of culture

In Molloys off-licence in Clondalkin last Saturday
night about eight o'clock.

This girl and her Ma came in. The Ma, of course,
was wearing her pyjamas and slippers. They
picked up a couple of bottles of Black Tower
and were looking at the crisps. The daughter
picks up a packet of fancy Thai spicy crisps with
pictures of red peppers on the bag.

'Wharrabouh dem, Ma?'

'Ah, no way. Dey look like dey'd burn yeh.'

Overheard by Austo, Molloys, Clondalkin
Posted on Monday, 16 October 2006

Monkey magic on the no. 10 bus

After waiting over 45 minutes on the NCR for a no. 10 from the Phoenix Park, the bus finally pulls up to the stop. When the door opens the old woman, a real Dub, at the front of the queue says to the driver,

'What were ye doin up there? Feedin' the bleedin' monkeys!'

The driver replies, 'Yeah, and takin' on some bleedin' monkeys as well!'

Only in Dublin!

Overheard by Joxer, North Circular Road
Posted on Friday, 13 October 2006

A T-ahem

Waiting in an ATM queue on Georges Street one weekend and one person seems to be taking quite a long time to use the machine. Man behind me shouts up to the girl at the machine,

'What are you gettin up there, a bleedin' mortgage!'

Overheard by Seán, Georges Street
Posted on Friday, 13 October 2006

Only something a Dub would say!

The day of the Liffey Swim a few weeks back, my
friends and I were heading in to town on the
no. 25A bus. Of course everyone was curious to
see what was happening, so whilst stuck in
traffic on the quays this Dublin girl got up and
went over to the other side of the bus to see
what everyone was staring at.

She turned around and said to her boyfriend
(and everyone else on the bus),

'Jeysus, one a dem is gonna get stuck in a
bleeding shopping trolley!'

Overheard by Penelope, on the no. 25A bus
Posted on Wednesday, 11 October 2006

That rhino's bleedin' sweatin!

Overheard by a friend of mine, who was recently
at a circus on the northside of Dublin. Show was
in full swing, animals and everything, including
a rhino which was mounted by one of the
performers.

Beside him was a young couple. Conversation is
as follows:

Young one: 'That's f**king horrible!'

Young fella: 'What is?'

Young one: 'Him riding that rhino, it's bleedin'
sweating!'

Overheard by Moz, at the circus
Posted on Wednesday, 11 October 2006

Making it up?

Overheard the announcer on an open-top Dublin Tour bus going by Burdock's chipper.

'To your right we have Burdock's, Dublin's most famous fish and chip shop. An array of celebrities have eaten in this famous chip shop, from Molly Malone right up to U2.'

Molly Malone?

Overheard by Willy, Werburgh Street
Posted on Tuesday, 10 October 2006

Off da ...

Crowd of young lads sitting in McDonald's, possibly just back from a trip to the US, or maybe just talking about a DVD they'd seen. Phrases such as 'off da hook' and 'off da ...' one thing and the other etc. are being bandied about.

The analyst of the group pronounces, 'Off da hook is the most famous of all the offdas.'

Overheard by Mozzer, McDonald's, Ranelagh
Posted on Monday, 9 October 2006

The joy of childbirth

A while back the sister-in-law of a mate of mine had her first child. It was a big baby and had to be delivered by Caesarean section. I'm translating here, because the text I got from my mate read:

'She had a baby boy this morning. Big fella. Came out the sun roof.'

Overheard by Diego, by text
Posted on Monday, 9 October 2006

Top prize?

Watching the Ireland versus Cyprus game on Saturday in the Bankers pub in town.

Coming near the end of the game, Ireland losing 5-2, the commentator says that after the game they will be doing their 'Man of the Match' competition. He said, 'The top prize is two tickets to Ireland's next match.'

Cue somebody shouts out,

'Yeah more a f**kin' booby prize!'

Overheard by Mac, Bankers in town
Posted on Monday, 9 October 2006

A G.S.O.H. essential

Two scobie types sitting on the no. 78A bus behind me, talking about a pet dog they used to have.

Scobie 1: 'Ye'd miss him around though, wouldn't ye?'

Scobie 2: 'Ah yea, he was a mad little b*stard, wasn't he?'

Scobie 1: 'Yeah. D'ya remember the time he left a shite on the bed and then when you were cleaning it he took another shite on the floor?'

Scobie 2: 'Yeah, he was gas . . .'

Overheard by Sue, on the no. 78A bus
Posted on Thursday, 5 October 2006

Rural resettlement

Picked up two women in my taxi in Ballymun. One asked to go to the City Council buildings at Wood Quay. They got talking on the way in, and one says to the other,

'Jaysus, I'm going in here to see about rural resettlement. I'm goin to tell them I want a dormant bungalow in Carlow, no upstairs ...'

Overheard by Terry, in my taxi
Posted on Tuesday, 3 October 2006

True love

On the no. 150 bus going into town, a drunk couple get on and sit down the back. A few minutes pass, then the guy stands up and shouts, 'Excuse me, ladies and gentleman, I'd just like to say I love this woman!'

The woman turns her head away from him and says, 'Ah jaysus, will ye stop, you're makin' me scarlet!'

And he says, 'Shut up, ye stupid bitch!'

Overheard by JohnG, on the no. 150 bus
Posted on Monday, 2 October 2006

Where's de justice in dat?

One day while working in Dun Laoghaire Shopping Centre, one annoyed 'head-the-ball' comes running up to one of the security guards and screams at him,

'Yer man is down there accusing me of robbin …'

The security guard looks back and the 'head-the-ball' says,

'… I wouldn't mind but I haven't robbed in here in weeks!'

Overheard by Cobs, Dun Laoghaire Shopping Centre
Posted on Friday, 29 September 2006

Never get a rickshaw in Dublin

I was getting on a rickshaw (drunk) going back to a girl's house one Saturday evening. We were in a passionate embrace and full of lust. As we passed a couple of lads on a corner, one of them shouted, 'De ye's want a knife and fork!'

Overheard by Karl, Rathmines
Posted on Thursday, 28 September 2006

Lost and found?

Overseen actually. Was walking past the Bleeding Horse on Camden Street when my boyfriend brought my attention to a small sticker on a lamp-post:

'Lost nail clippers, this is urgent, you have no idea how long my toe-nails are, information, please contact …'

You can see it for yourselves, it's on a lamp-post near the smoking area on the street!

Overheard by Leona, outside the Bleeding Horse

Posted on Wednesday, 27 September 2006

Can I take your order?

A drunk goes into the local chipper after a few scoops and orders a shark burger and chips. The disgruntled worker ignores him but the man keeps shouting up his order. Eventually the chippy shouts back, 'We don' do dem!'

Your man responds, 'Ye don' do dem? Just a shark burger so!'

Overheard by Larry, northside chipper

Posted on Wednesday, 27 September 2006

Final destination

As the Luas was approaching the Red Cow, there was the following announcement over the loudspeaker:

'All passengers will be terminated at Abbey Street.'

Overheard by Helen, Luas (Red Cow)

Posted on Wednesday, 27 September 2006

Show must go on

Queuing for a p*ss in the pub, drunk guy at urinal beside me announces, 'I have stage fright. I can't go, and I am bursting!'

Overheard by Paul, The Old Mill pub, Tallaght
Posted on Monday, 25 September 2006

What's the craic

In passport control coming back from Thailand, my boy's passport had been stolen by a prostitute. He only had an emergency passport from the embassy (which was a green piece of paper, might I add).

The passport officer kindly told us, 'Believe me, it will turn up in a few days with a foreigner coming through in an Ireland jersey, asking me what the craic is!'

Overheard by Anonymous, Dublin Airport
Posted on Friday, 22 September 2006

Balanced diet

A young boy and his mother in the Centra in Bray. The young lad picks up a carton of milk and when seen by his mother is told to, 'Put it back, don't you know you are having a can of coke with your chips!'

Overheard by Barney, Centra, Bray
Posted on Thursday, 21 September 2006

800-year struggle

Spray-painted on a wall at the entrance of my mate's estate in Donabate:

'BIRTS OUT!'

It's been there for years, uncorrected!

Overheard by Rory, Donabate
Posted on Wednesday, 20 September 2006

Euclid would be proud

I was on the ferry from Holyhead to Dun Laoghaire and I got talking with an ould pair from Limerick. It was the first time they had travelled abroad. The ould one said to me,

'We usually go on holidays to Lahinch. It's grand. It's only 50 miles from home and only 50 miles back again.'

Overheard by John, Stena Line ferry
Posted on Wednesday, 20 September 2006

Talking fruit

Girl: 'So where are you from, you sound Australian?'

Guy: 'Wales, but I do have a bit of a kiwi accent.'

Girl (laughing hysterically): 'What?! Kiwis can't talk!'

Overheard by Anonymous, St Stephen's Green
Posted on Monday, 18 September 2006

EU or not EU

Arriving recently at passport control in Dublin Airport, I overheard two English girls debating whether they should be in the queue 'EU' or 'Non-EU'.

'I was never very good at geography in school,' one of them said, 'so I don't know if England is in the EU or not.'

'Well, we don't have the euro,' the other one replied, 'so we mustn't be.'

They then joined the non-EU queue.

Overheard by Sean, Dublin Airport
Posted on Monday, 18 September 2006

Small change

Got on the bus a couple of weeks ago, having decided to get rid of all the small coins in my change jar at home. I poured my €1.35 fare, all in coppers, into the machine.

'Robbin' the piggy bank again?' asked the bus driver.

'Something like that,' I laughed.

'Or else,' he said, grinning, 'you must be a terrible singer.'

Overheard by Aoibhlinn, on the no. 18 bus
Posted on Monday, 18 September 2006

Unhappy customer

On the crowded no. 39 bus from the city to Blanch at rush hour.

A little girl of maybe four years kept screaming and crying. Her mother was wondering what was bothering her.

'Why are you so upset?'

The little bugger replied, 'Mommy, I hate f**kin' Dublin Bus.'

Overheard by Mr Winterbottom, on the no. 39 bus
Posted on Saturday, 16 September 2006

Irish Superbowl

On a recent flight from New York to Dublin, three elderly Yanks had the following discussion:

Yank 1: 'I believe it's Superbowl weekend in Ireland next weekend.' (clearly talking about the upcoming All-Ireland football final)

Yank 2: 'Wow, they play (American) football in Ireland?'

Yank 1: 'No, Irish football.'

Yank 3: 'You mean soccer?'

Yank 1: 'No, Irish football, they play with a rugby-shaped ball and wear loads of padding.'

Had to bite my lip!

Overheard by Staffy, on a flight from New York to Dublin
Posted on Friday, 15 September 2006

Language barriers

A Dub in work is queuing for a sandwich. As it's being made up, he's answering all the questions — in pure Dub — from a Polish girl, who is using what English she has to try and

understand what he wants. She's wearing a
completely baffled expression because she has
no idea what this fella is saying, but carries on as
best she can:

'You want lettuce?'

'That's deadly!' (adds lettuce).

'Tomato?'

'Nice one … tomato' (adds tomato).

'Ok, you want mayonnaise or salad cream?'

'Aw sure, it's legend as it is.'

The Polish girl tries to put mayo on, to cries
from Auld Dub, 'Nah, nah, it's legend, legend!'

Overheard by Anonymous, working in Dublin
Posted on Thursday, 14 September 2006

A Dub in London Zoo

At London Zoo, my friend's sister passes by an
enclosure under construction. A Portakabin
behind a fence had Mifflin & Co. printed on a
yellow sticker near the roof of the cabin. She
calls over her two kids,

'Tom and Liam, come and see the mifflins!'

Overheard by David, London Zoo
Posted on Thursday, 14 September 2006

I'll be back

A non-national was hit by a vehicle at the
pedestrian crossing on O'Connell Street. It was a
minor accident, but looked all the more
dramatic as he rolled off the bonnet of the car

and continued walking briskly away. Cue a
stunned Howya at the lights:

'Jaysus, it's the bleeding Terminator!'

Overheard by Vincent, O'Connell Street
Posted on Thursday, 14 September 2006

Time to go home

When I was leaving Electric Picnic on the
Monday morning, a guy ahead of me said, 'You
know you've been here too long when you start
dancing to the sound of the generators!'

Overheard by Síle, Electric Picnic
Posted on Wednesday, 13 September 2006

Mental

My friend and I were sitting in a park having a
cigarette, when an old drunken man approaches

us, asking for a 'spare smoke'.

Myself, whilst taking out a cigarette: 'I must warn you, they're menthol.'

Drunk: 'Ah, sure oim mental meself!'

Overheard by Creem, Ranelagh Gardens
Posted on Monday, 11 September 2006

Staying level headed

Going over the DART tracks on the upper floor of the no. 32 bus, it rocks and bounces over them, swaying dangerously. Old man who was trying to stand up gets pushed back into his seat by the movement, and mutters, 'Level crossing me HOLE!'

Overheard by Denis, on the no. 32 bus
Posted on Friday, 8 September 2006

Terms of endearment

Walking down Henry Street, two young Dublin women chatting to each other while trying to keep their various kids from running too far ahead.

One woman hands her couple-of-months-old baby to the other in order to chase a toddler who is trying a great escape, with the immortal words:

'Hold this bundle o' f**ks, while I clatter yer man.'

Overheard by Zara, Henry Street
Posted on Wednesday, 6 September 2006

Irish terror alert level

The day after the latest 'terror plot' panic in Britain, my Dad overheard a passenger who was waiting to board the ferry at Dun Laoghaire ask a harbour policeman,

'What state of alert are yis on?'

Quick as a flash the harbour policeman says, 'Barely awake.'

Overheard by Dub, Stena terminal, Dun Laoghaire
Posted on Tuesday, 5 September 2006

Anaesthesia! Bless you!

A few years ago, I had occasion to be in the casualty department of Blanchardstown Hospital, getting a cut stitched, as was the 'jaysis-howaya' chap in the next cubicle. He was being treated by a doctor of Asian origin, who had a very strong accent.

The youngfella says to the doctor as treatment started, 'Eh, d'ye moind if I don' look, pal?' to which the doctor says, 'Certainly.'

A blood-curdling scream followed, as well as every type of expletive you can think up. After this died down, the nurse that was treating me calmly called through the curtain,

'He said do you mind if I don't LOOK, not do you mind if I don't have a LOCAL!'

Overheard by Stillsick, James Connolly Hospital, A&E
Posted on Monday, 4 September 2006

Welcome to Ireland

An African gets on the no. 83 bus on Westmoreland Street, flashes his travel pass at the driver and sits down.

An auld one beside me says, '… and they've got the free travel as well …'

Overheard by Niall, on the no. 83 bus
Posted on Monday, 4 September 2006

The thin white line

My sister was driving to Dublin in the car and my father was the front-seat passenger; in the back was my three-year-old nephew. He suddenly asks, 'Mam, what are the white lines in the middle of the road for?'

My father and sister both explain the reason for white lines in the middle of the road.

There is silence in the back.

A couple of minutes later the nephew pipes up, 'But what happens when it snows?'

Overheard by Tappers, off me skin and blister
Posted on Sunday, 3 September 2006

Jesus was a joker

Two years ago when I was working in the city centre I used to meet a friend for lunch on the steps of St Mary's Pro-cathedral just off Marlborough Street (classy, I know!). So we'd sit there chatting and laughing our heads off, a little bit down from the main door where people would come out of Mass. So one day this old disgruntled pensioner woman comes over to scold us:

'You young wans have no respect, stop your laughing, this is a house of God!'

To which another woman says, 'Ah don't mind her, sure didn't Jesus enjoy a bit of messin in his day!'

Overheard by Liz, Marlborough Street
Posted on Wednesday, 30 August 2006

Get this man an atlas!

Some scumbag had been caught red-handed trying to lift cans out of the Centra/Spar at O'Connell Bridge by a 6' 10" security guard, clearly of African origin. Amidst the barrage of abuse he uttered whilst being ejected from the shop, he shouted,

'Get away from me, you big f**kin' Albanian asylum seeker b**tard, ye!'

Overheard by Hugh, Westmoreland Street
Posted on Wednesday, 30 August 2006

Love has its 'benefits'

Written on the sign at the front of the Social Welfare office on Tara Street:

'Noelle Call Me'

Only Dublin …

Overheard by Andy, Tara Street
Posted on Wednesday, 30 August 2006

Not such an easy pass

Driving down towards the M50 toll bridge with my Dad (in my sister's car, using her Eazy Pass). As my Dad pulls up to the barrier, he holds up the Eazy Pass in front of him. Nothing happens! He's going mad pointing the Eazy Pass in all directions, all over the windscreen. Still the barrier never moves.

He rolls down the window, says to the young lad in the booth, 'This poxy thing's not workin,' to which the young lad replies, 'Hold it up behind the rear view mirror, barcode facing out!'

My dad follows his instructions and — hey presto — the barrier lifts. Then the young lad says,

'Now you see dat, mister, they're Eazy Passes, not feckin' remotes!'

Overheard by Martin, M50 toll bridge
Posted on Monday, 28 August 2006

Cat tranquillisers

On the no. 7 bus coming through Sallynoggin, two lads sitting at the back of the bus with a cat:

'Where did ya get da cat?'

'I stroked it off me aunty.'

'For what?'

'Gonna take it to da mobile vet in Tesco car park and tell the vet the fecker's depressed, ye can get animal tranquillisers off them, piece of piss.'

'Ah yeah, nice one!'

This conversation went on for another five minutes — with the top of the bus in hysterics (under their breath of course)!

Overheard by Anonymous, on the no. 7 bus
Posted on Friday, 25 August 2006

More like Thick Lizzy

At a Thin Az Lizzy gig. Girl behind me mutters to her boyfriend (obviously didn't want to be there),

'Yeah, they are good, but why are they only playing Thin Lizzy stuff?'

… errr?

Overheard by Jimmy, Whelan's on Wexford Street
Posted on Thursday, 24 August 2006

Disability of Laziness

I was on the no. 77A bus one day, coming home from town. There was a foreigner selling newspapers at the traffic lights.

Two lads down the back, one of them comments, 'Jayz, you'd think he'd get a decent job like, ya know.'

The other one replies, 'What are you saying, you haven't even got a f**kin' job!'

'Yea well … I … I have a disability!'

Overheard by David, on the no. 77A bus
Posted on Wednesday, 23 August 2006

A taxi driver who cares

A friend of mine had just arrived home after a year studying abroad, and was in a taxi heading to town from Rathmines one summer evening. He had rolled down the window to get some air.

Coming down Wexford Street, traffic was slow as a lot of people were gathered outside Whelan's/ The Village and some had spilled onto the road.

As the taxi passed the crowd, someone reached into the car and slapped my mate across the face. As if this wasn't injury enough, after a few seconds the clearly unconcerned but amused driver enquired,

'Got a bit of a slap there, did ya?'

I'm not usually a fan of taxi drivers, but this one deserves a round of applause for his compassion …

Overheard by Dan, Wexford Street
Posted on Tuesday, 22 August 2006

Crystal balls

A friend of mine was getting on a no. 11 bus on O'Connell Street when a lady boarded, obviously irate at having waited so long. She asked the driver when the next no. 10 would be along. Quick as a shot, the driver turned to her and said,

'Missus, I've got two balls, unfortunately neither of them are crystal.'

Apparently this satisfied the lady and off she got,

laughing her head off!

Overheard by Kevin, on the no. 11 bus
Posted on Monday, 21 August 2006

Top quality food

I was in McDonald's with a few friends last week. One of my friends says, 'I'll have a milkshake and six nuggets please', to which the cashier replies, 'What flavour would you like?'

Quick as a flash, my other friend says, 'Chicken!'

The group of us cracked up laughing ... cashier didn't seem amused though.

Overheard by Anonymous, McDonald's, Stillorgan
Posted on Monday, 21 August 2006

Best birthday ever!

On the day of the infamous Dublin riots, I was crossing O'Connell Bridge when I passed two lads fresh from battle with the Gardaí (and presumably on their way to Leinster House). I overheard one say to the other,

'Jayse, Anto, this is the best birthday ya ever had!'

Overheard by Dan, O'Connell Bridge
Posted on Saturday, 19 August 2006

Advanced linguistics

Junior Cert French class, the fellow sitting in front of me turned around and started telling me about some match he'd been to at weekend, swearing every second word.

'Yeah, it was mad sh*t, the f**kin' defence was all over the f**kin' shop, they …'

'Jason, stand up!' the teacher says, 'How dare you use that language in my classroom!'

Jason turns around, genuinely outraged:

'What language? English?! Just 'cos it's a French class, we can't speak English?'

Overheard by Jay, Junior Cert French class
Posted on Friday, 18 August 2006

Super disturbing taxi driver

In a taxi the other day with a few friends. The Dubliner driver must have been 20 stone at least. Somehow the conversation turns to beds. Driver starts telling us that he's got a water bed at home. Cue a lot of, 'Oh right, what's that like then?' trying hard not to picture him.

After that he says, 'Ah, you have to try different things … y'know … experiment, like, did you ever try jumping off the wardrobe?'

Cue laughter as this sinks in, yet another disturbing sight.

'Yeah, jumping off the wardrobe, wearing a superman outfit, ya hafta try it.'

Man, we were in fits coming out of that cab. I hope he was joking, that poor woman …

Overheard by K, in a Dublin taxi
Posted on Tuesday, 15 August 2006

Would only happen in Dublin

About two months ago while getting the no. 27 bus home, I saw a 'head-the-ball' sitting upstairs at the back of the bus. He had an X-ray in his hands and was holding it up to the window, looking at it very curiously.

I hear some fluttering, and he was examining a totally different X-ray.

Hmmm, I began to grow curious and moved a seat or two back.

He had a pile of them, I could only guess 60+.

That's what I love about Dublin. A guy wanders into some hospital, decides he would like something to play with on the ride home, and tada — he has it!

Overheard by Graham, on the no. 27 bus
Posted on Thursday, 10 August 2006

The state of Kilbarrack

Was getting the no. 29A bus at Eden Quay the other day when two of our American friends boarded. The gentleman asked the driver, 'Excuse me, sir, where this does bus go?'

To which the driver replied, 'Kilbarrack, Bud.'

The American gentleman then enquired, 'What state is that in?'

To which our Dublin Bus hero replied, 'It's in an awful bleedin' state, mister.'

Overheard by Keith, on the no. 29A bus at Eden Quay
Posted on Tuesday, 8 August 2006

Six stabs = alrigh?

Young wan: 'How's Decco?'

Young fella: 'He's alrigh, got out of James's Monday.'

Young wan: 'What happened him?'

Young fella: 'Six stabs in the chest — he's alrigh — lucky b**tard.'

Overheard by Nicantuile, Tallaght
Posted on Sunday, 6 August 2006

Someone needs to spend more time in the office!

In Brown Thomas the other day looking at Chloé bags, and called over an official-looking woman to verify a price. Woman comes over and tells us a particular bag is €478.50, and €1,032 in the same colour but with a metallic sheen.

We ask why is it nearly double for a metallic colour and she launches into a big long discussion about it being this, that and the other and 'special metallic effect' and 'nearly impossible to get from any other designer'.

Then the husband came up behind her and asked if she was ready to go!

Couldn't believe she didn't even work there!

Overheard by Raychelle, Brown Thomas, Grafton Street

Posted on Friday, 4 August 2006

Hairy legs

Was in River Island on Grafton Street last week with my six-year-old niece, paying for a pair of jeans. The little brat roars out in front of a very long queue:

'Why are you buying jeans with holes in the legs of them? Sure isn't everyone going to see your hairy legs?!'

Overheard by Anonymous, River Island on Grafton Street

Posted on Wednesday, 2 August 2006

Animal noises

In Dublin Zoo last year I was walking by the farm animals. A little girl (about six) ran by us. Her Ma noticed a sheep and called after her daughter,

'Look, Kelly, a sheep ... moo ... or baah, whatever ...'

Overheard by Joey, Dublin Zoo

Posted on Tuesday, 1 August 2006

Destiny's Child

Walking past a chipper on Faussagh Avenue, Cabra, I overheard two young girls, aged about eleven, discussing one of their sisters:

'Ah sure me sister's been in a right mood since the wedding was called off, her Beyonce was doin the dirt on her!'

Overheard by Karen, Faussagh Avenue, Cabra
Posted on Sunday, 30 July 2006

Nuns looking for heaven

I was walking down Nassau Street. Outside the Kilkenny Showrooms, there were two elderly nuns in habit, and an elderly lady looking at what appeared to be a street map. Just at that moment a middle-aged man, scruffy looking, came out of the shop, looked at the group, and spontaneously shouted across to them,

'What are you's looking for? The way to heaven?'

I laughed all the way back to work!

Overheard by Domer, outside the Kilkenny Showrooms
Posted on Thursday, 27 July 2006

Jaysis Jesus

Looking for a flat block in Dolphin's Barn complex and stopped a local man, asking, 'Can you tell me where flat 32G is, please?'

He responds, 'Is that G as in Jesus or J as in jaysis?'

Overheard by Erica, Dolphin's Barn
Posted on Thursday, 20 July 2006

Bitten on the Supermacs

I was getting the bus in from the airport and sitting in front of me were two D4 girls, one telling the other about her friend who was attacked by a dog (or loike a massive wolf, as she put it). She said,

'And then the wolf cornered him and, loike, jumped on him and knocked him over, then it started biting him.'

Her mate goes, 'Oh my God! Where did it bite him?'

D4 girl: 'Outside Supermacs.'

Overheard by Ian, airport bus
Posted on Wednesday, 19 July 2006

Eagle-eye cops!

I was at the Dublin versus Offaly match, and just after a steward got hit with a bottle, I overheard two Gardaí talking. One pointed to the stands and said,

'Yer man there in the Dublin top threw the bottle!'

Overheard by Steve, Croke Park
Posted on Monday, 17 July 2006

It's a long way to the top!

On Hill 16 for the Dublin versus Offaly match, group of lads come along looking for a good spot to stand. Guy leading the group keeps going up higher towards the back, when one of the lads shouts out,

'For f**k's sake, we're not on a sponsored walk!'

Overheard by Anonymous, Hill 16
Posted on Sunday, 16 July 2006

Who needs the bank manager?

Guy looking for cash on the lane beside The George, lots of punters passing by in the evening. The usual, 'Any spare change?' to which I'm ashamed to say, you normally walk on.

Then, just as you reach this particular guy, he asks, 'Any chance of a loan of €50?'

I cracked up laughing. Gave him whatever change I had (well over a fiver) and he thanked me very much — before pointing out that it was 'grand' if I couldn't rise to a 50!

Overheard by M, Georges Street
Posted on Thursday, 13 July 2006

Results!

In school, our maths teacher was asking what results we got in our Christmas exams. He gets around to asking my mate who is clearly daydreaming:

Teacher: 'What did you get at Christmas?'

Mate: 'Liverpool jersey and a watch, Sir!'

Overheard by Daz, Ardscoil Rís, Griffith Avenue
Posted on Thursday, 13 July 2006

Weights and measures

Scruffy 'arty' type punter: 'Two pints of Carlsberg, one with four inches of white lemonade and the other with one inch of white lemonade.'

Old style grumpy/sardonic Dublin barman: 'No problem, I have me measuring tape out the back.'

Overheard by DB, the Leeson Lounge
Posted on Wednesday, 12 July 2006

Small folk

My cousin's four-year-old daughter is very smart and quick to pass comment loudly in public. She was sitting on the bus with her mother when a male midget wearing sports gear got on and sat across the aisle from them. My cousin warned her daughter not to say anything, even though this was the first time she had seen a midget.

The little girl would not be frustrated, though, and after thinking about it for a few moments, said for all on the bus to hear,

'Mammy, that's the smallest tracksuit I've ever seen!'

Overheard by Erica, on the no. 10 bus
Posted on Wednesday, 12 July 2006

Free tour

Upstairs on the no. 38 bus coming into town. Old Dublin dear with headscarf, brown mac and sensible shoes, sitting behind a very tanned young girl with long black hair.

As we go by any landmark, the old dear leans slightly forward and whispers its name fairly loudly, 'The Phoenix Park', 'St Peter's Church', 'The Garden of Remembrance'. Girl is getting narked and finally turns round to old dear and says,

'I'm not a bleedin' foreigner! I just have a tan from me holidays!'

Overheard by Erica, on the no. 38 bus
Posted on Monday, 10 July 2006

KFnoChicken

About a year ago I went into KFC at lunchtime and asked for some sort of chicken meal. The assistant told me, 'We have no chicken today!'

KFC with no chicken … could only happen in Ireland!

Overheard by Nicola, KFC
Posted on Monday, 10 July 2006

A dishy name

My grandmother, a real Dub!

On the birth of my daughter Sorcha (pronounced Sorsha):

'You're calling her what?'

'Saucer! What sort of name is that for a little girl, she will never forgive you!'

Overheard by Paul, my Nan's house, Portmarnock
Posted on Monday, 10 July 2006

Little brown girl

A few years ago there was a street party on my road. A woman was dancing with a load of children in a ring! In the middle of the ring was a little black girl. The woman enthusiastically began to sing,

'Brown girl in the ring, tra-la-la-la-la ...'

She suddenly realised what she was singing, quickly stopped and went bright red!

Overheard by Will, Donnycarney
Posted on Sunday, 9 July 2006

I pity the fool ...

In Down Under at Stephen's Green, wearing a 'Mr T' t-shirt with a picture of the man himself saying, 'Ain't got no time fo jibba-jabba', or some such catchphrase.

A girl approaches me by the bar, looks at the t-shirt and says,

'So you're a big Mike Tyson fan?'

Overheard by Ciaran, Down Under bar, St Stephen's Green

Posted on Friday, 7 July 2006

Free-range

Middle-aged woman asks vegetable stall-holder on Moore Street,

'Are those onions free-range?'

Stall-holder looks at her and says,

'Yes, love, and I'm tellin' ye, they're very hard to catch!'

Overheard by Erica, Moore Street

Posted on Thursday, 6 July 2006

B.L.A.N.C.H.A.R.D.S.T.O.W.N.

Sitting in my car in southside retail park, two guys getting into car beside me. One has thick Dublin accent and the other guy was foreign:

Dublin Guy: 'No, we'll try Liffey Valley first.'

Foreign Guy: 'Not Blanchardstown?'

Dublin Guy: 'No, no, not Blanchardstown.'

Foreign Guy: 'Why not?'

Dublin Guy: 'Well … (trying to look for the words) … Blanchardstown is … eh … it's for (pronounced very carefully and slowly) s.c.u.m.b.a.g.s.'

The Dublin guy spots me smiling and, obviously worried, a minute later he goes,

'Excuse me, you're not from Blanchardstown are you?'

For the record, I don't think Blanchardstown is for scumbags (I reckon he just didn't fancy going through the toll!).

Overheard by Jo, Liffey Valley

Posted on Thursday, 6 July 2006

VH-not impressed

I was in ExtraVision a while back and two girls came in asking the chap behind the counter whether he sold video cassettes for a camera. The bloke gave them a withering look and said, 'No'.

'Well, do you know where we can get some?' say the girls.

'Try the 80s,' says the bloke as he turns his back.

Nice!

Overheard by Mugwumpjism, ExtraVision, Coolock

Posted on Tuesday, 4 July 2006

Muppetry

I was waiting to get on the bus on Dame Street, feeling slightly under the influence. The bus pulls up and the guy in front of me waves a €5 note and tries to stick it into the coin machine. The bus driver looks past him, directly at me and says, 'Once a muppet always a muppet, that's what I always say!'

Overheard by Cole, Dame Street

Posted on Saturday, 1 July 2006

Foul-mouthed toddler

Walking into the Square in Tallaght yesterday, I was met by a woman walking backwards shouting, 'I'm leav-EN, come on Way-EN,' as she went out the door. I had a look to see who she was shouting at, and spotted a young lad of about two or three, starting to run all the way back at the escalators.

As he started to run, he began that frightened crying that only a lost child can do, and began roaring.

As he came closer I finally made out what he was saying:

'Fer f**k sake, MA! Fer f**k sake, MA!' … over and over.

Everyone within earshot was in knots!

Overheard by Ross, The Squa-AH
Posted on Friday, 30 June 2006

Not a fan of ice-cream

Picture this. Stuck in traffic on Amiens Street on a roasting hot day in June — going nowhere. Some poxy truck hit a car. I had the car windows down, getting some air. About four or five young ones were standing at a doorway across the road.

One had just thrown water at the others and there was the usual talk of, 'Tracey, ya b*ll*x!' etc.

I spotted this guy walking towards them and he was eating the biggest ice-cream I've ever seen. It looked like the ice-cream seller had thrown about eight scoops onto his cone.

As he walked passed, one of the girls shouts out,

'Here, youngfella, give us a lick of your balls!'

Overheard by Damo, on Amiens Street
Posted on Thursday, 29 June 2006

Health care crisis

Standing on Hill 16 during the Meath versus Dublin Leinster Championship game in 2005 when Meath pariah Graham Geraghty fell to the ground, badly injured. The motorised stretcher thing came to pick him up, and as he was being carted away in obvious pain to a chorus of BEE-BAH BEE-BAH, a little gurrier of no more than seven leapt up from behind me and roared,

'I hope you're waiting on a f**kin' bed!'

Overheard by Hally, Croke Park
Posted on Thursday, 29 June 2006

Extra time at the Ireland v. Chile game

Chile were winning 1-0, and it was coming towards the end of the game. The announcement came over the loudspeaker that there would be something ridiculous like six minutes of extra time (an unusual amount for a friendly game).

Anyhow, as it was announced, two typical Dubs were passing:

'Jaysus, Thommo, six minutes? He must be adding that much time for when we went for burgers!'

Overheard by John, Lansdowne Road
Posted on Wednesday, 28 June 2006

Cut down to size

Having a pint in Kehoes off Grafton Street. Quiet time, when three loud Americans come in from golf. Loudest guy is 6 foot 5 inches and is flanked by two nearly-7-footers. He says to the barmaid, 'These guys are nearly 7 foot tall, and I am 6 foot 5. Guess what they call me?'

Without drawing breath she replies,

'Billie Bob.'

Cue sniggering … and a return to the quiet of the pub.

Pure class. Wish I was that quick!

Overheard by Mark, Kehoes off Grafton Street
Posted on Tuesday, 27 June 2006

Moving statue

My mate and I were killing time by watching one of the human statue street performers on Grafton Street. Just as we were about to push off, a gruff voice came from the back,

'He'd move if you ran off with his box!'

Lovely stuff!

Overheard by Shane M, Grafton Street
Posted on Wednesday, 28 June 2006

Knowing where your priorities lie

(Irate) girl on mobile: '… So you're telling me I can't see you until after the World Cup?'

Overheard by Anonymous, St Stephen's Green
Posted on Friday, 23 June 2006

While Heimlich turns in his grave

While in the Cherry Tree pub recently, a man started to cough while eating peanuts. His female companion panicked and shouted,

'Quickly — somebody use the Heineken Manoeuvre!'

Overheard by Dick, Cherry Tree pub, Walkinstown
Posted on Wednesday, 21 June 2006

Miss Education

Walking around Dublin Zoo, the year the safari park part opened, on a very hot Sunday with loads of families about. It just happened to be feeding time when we were walking by the seal

area, and people had begun to gather around to watch the feeding.

A large crane landed on one of the boulders in the middle of the pool and a small boy pointed to the crane and asked his mother, 'What's tha'?'

The mother says with a big smile on her face, 'Oh tha', tha's a boird!'

God love the yout!

Overheard by Kate, Dublin Zoo
Posted on Wednesday, 21 June 2006

Space knickers

I started working in Dublin Airport recently. While talking to my supervisor, a group of Ryanair air hostesses passed by. I enquired if the airport staff mingled with the airline's hostesses. His reply was,

'Ah yeah, the Ryanair girls are sound, but the Aer Lingus girls must have space knickers on 'cos they think their fanny is out of this world.'

Overheard by Dav, Dublin Airport
Posted on Friday, 16 June 2006

The fashion

Two old dears talking on the no. 19A bus last night:

Old dear #1: 'Do you see the kids in the runners these days?'

Old dear #2: 'I do, yeah.'

Old dear #1: 'The thing they do now is they put the laces into the runners.'

Old dear #2: 'They don't?'

Old dear #1: 'They do!'

Old dear #2: 'Do they?'

Old dear #1: 'They do. It's the fashion.'

Old dear #2: 'They don't tie them?'

Old dear #1: 'They don't. Just put the laces into the runners.'

Old dear #2: 'That's the fashion, I suppose.'

Overheard by Shango, on the no. 19A bus
Posted on Friday, 16 June 2006

That's not HELP!

When I was waiting for the train in Connolly Station, my insanely bushy-haired friend had his bag stolen. He anxiously runs to the help desk:

'I'm sorry but my bag has been stolen.'

The person behind the desk smirks and replies,

'Did it contain a hairbrush?'

My friend stares at her, not amused.

Overheard by Donal, Connolly Station
Posted on Friday, 16 June 2006

Attention to detail

Was watching the start of the Italy versus Ghana match, when my Mum walks into the room. One or two of the Ghana players had tops with 'Germany '06' written on the front. Mum spots this and pipes up:

'Isn't that great, look at the German team, they're all black.'

Overheard by Richie, at home while watching the World Cup
Posted on Thursday, 15 June 2006

Religious bankers

While walking behind three office types toward the Green, I overheard them talking about the office:

Banker #1: 'How's work these days?'

Banker #2: 'You know the story in the Bible about the man who was being constantly annoyed at home? He went to a wise man for advice and was told to get a goat and to keep it in the house. The goat made a load of noise and a major mess so things got worse. The man went back to the wise man to complain, and was told to get rid of the goat. Once the goat was gone things didn't seem so bad. Well, the goat's on holidays.'

I think we've all been there …

Overheard by Mike, Baggot Street
Posted on Thursday, 15 June 2006

She's lovely

I was in a petrol station one day when a bunch of students came in. There was a bit of a queue forming as we were all waiting for the cashier to reappear from the back.

Anyway, I overheard one of the students boasting to his mates: 'You should see the one who works in here, she is f**kin' lovely.'

Just then the cashier comes into the front of the shop. He is fat, bald and in his 50s. The other students turn around and say,

'Oh yeah, she's a f**king stunner.'

Overheard by John, Bray
Posted on Thursday, 15 June 2006

Romance lives

One night, watching a movie with Brad Pitt in it.

My mother says, 'Ooh, I wouldn't throw him out of bed for eating nuts,' to which my dad replies,

'If he was in bed with you, he *would* be nuts!'

Romance lives!

Overheard by Lorraine, at home
Posted on Wednesday, 14 June 2006

Patience of a prisoner

My friend worked as an electrician in Mountjoy Prison and heard this one morning. There is a shop in there which is open to the prisoners. One morning the shop was late opening, and as the shopkeeper came along to open it, a prisoner shouts from his jail cell,

'About f**kin' time, I've been waiting ages!'

Overheard by Derek, Mountjoy
Posted on Wednesday, 14 June 2006

No sugar coating required

In Swords, two women bump into each other.
One says,

'Jaysus, you're like our John — you're gone
HUGE!'

Overheard by Bridie, Swords
Posted on Tuesday, 13 June 2006

A solution to Africa's problems

While watching an ad for Concern, the voiceover
says, 'These people have to walk for three miles
every day just to get water,' to which my five-
year-old nephew replied,

'Why don't they just move closer to the water?'

Overheard by Derek, while watching TV at home
Posted on Monday, 12 June 2006

Miniature euros

I was getting fags in our local Spar for myself
and my pal Eve, when I decided to get a box of
chocolates for the pair of us. The chocs are
behind the counter so I asked the young cashier
for 'the big box of Miniature Heroes'.

She asked me what I wanted and I repeated,
pointing out where they were to the mystified
girl.

She walked over to the shelf, stared at it for a
few moments and mumbled something to the
other cashier, who kindly pointed them out to
her.

She returned red-faced, announcing:

'Ah, jaysus, I thought you asked for Miniature Euros, and I was sayin' to meself "What the f**k does she want them for?!"'

Overheard by Lainey, Spar, SCR
Posted on Thursday, 8 June 2006

Women's Mini Marathon

'Ow! I'm never doing that to anyone again!'

Man on having his bra strap pinged during the Women's Mini Marathon.

Overheard by Ann, 2006 Women's Mini Marathon
Posted on Tuesday, 6 June 2006

B and Queue

Standing in the queue for the till in B&Q last Saturday, buying a step-ladder. There's only three people in front of me, but it's taking the hapless cashier about ten minutes to deal with each customer, what with a dodgy scanner and barcodes not in the system.

As she left the till for the third or fourth time to ask a colleague what to do next, the bloke behind me looks at the one item I'm getting and says to me,

'Bet you wish you'd just stood on a f**kin' chair now!'

Overheard by Gary, B&Q, Liffey Valley
Posted on Tuesday, 6 June 2006

Ah yes, the charms of the Dublin taxi driver

I was standing outside Bewley's Hotel in Ballsbridge. There were three women nearby. A taxi pulled up and the driver got out. One of the women said to him, 'Are you a taxi?' to which he replied, pointing to his car,

'That's a taxi, luv, I'm a human being!'

Overheard by Áine, Bewley's Hotel, Ballsbridge
Posted on Monday, 5 June 2006

Excuse me, love ...

I was downstairs on the no. 78 bus a couple of months ago and spotted a young one talking happily away to herself. I thought, 'Ah, God love her,' until I realised she was using a hands-free phone.

Just then an oul' one leaned over to her and said,

'Excuse me, love, but yeh look like a feckin' eejit!'

The young one appeared mystified and slightly startled as the rest of us sniggered. She began to talk again to whoever was still on the phone, when the oul' one leaned over again and said,

'Excuse me, love, yeh didn't hear me. Yeh look like a feckin' eejit!'

Howls of laughter!

Overheard by Dave, on the no. 78 bus
Posted on Sunday, 4 June 2006

Shortage of smarts in ICU

A woman was talking vehemently to her friend about nurses in intensive care units:

'They just don't have the brain cells to know who's wellest.'

THEY are short on brain cells?!

Overheard by Anonymous, in a café in Glasnevin
Posted on Saturday, 3 June 2006

The lights are on but nobody's at home

My boss was assisting one of the shop-floor girls with the Christmas lights for the window, and they were having problems with the electrics. My boss went in the back to the fuse box, and called out to the girl,

'Well, are they workin' now?'

To which she replied,

'Oh, yeah! They're on now! … Oh … wait, off again … Oh, back on again!'

My boss could barely get out the words to explain to her the purpose of 'twinkling fairylights' …

Overheard by Alison, at work in Swords
Posted on Saturday, 3 June 2006

No sign of the directions

Came back to Dublin in January this year after many years away. Anyway, I couldn't find the DART station on Amiens Street (access is now different). I asked this guy working there for directions. I mention to him there are not many signs, to which he replies,

'Sure, we don't bother with signs as most people know where it is.'

Overheard by Anonymous, Amiens Street
Posted on Friday, 2 June 2006

The bouncer scale

One of a group of young-looking lads to the bouncers outside a lap-dancing club:

'So, on a scale of one to ten, how much am I not allowed in?'

Overheard by David O'C, outside Club Lapello on Dame Street
Posted on Friday, 2 June 2006

Dog's abuse

Dublin man to his dog, after it did a huge poo at the entrance of Trinity College:

'What are ya? … That's right, a fecking eejit!'

Overheard by Robin, outside Trinity College
Posted on Thursday, 1 June 2006

The singer

An ould drunk on the DART on Saturday evening, trying to convince some Dutch tourists to sing with him:

'I'm a singer,

Sure my whole family were singers,

My mother was a singer,

My father was a singer,

Even the sewing machine was a Singer …'

Overheard by Ruairi, on the DART
Posted on Tuesday, 30 May 2006

Wha's up?!?

In HMV Henry Street yesterday and there were two very white lads, about sixteen or seventeen years old, in the middle of doing an unnecessarily complicated handshake. As I walked by them, they finished and one said to the other,

'Right! Now we're black.'

Overheard by NM, HMV on Henry Street
Posted on Tuesday, 30 May 2006

You don't rip off an old lady

I was standing outside Clery's, waiting for a bus.
Beside me was an oul' one (in her 70s) with one
of them shopping bags on wheels. She was
staring into Clery's window and shaking her
head. She looked up at me and pointed at a hat
in the window.

'Who the feck would pay tha' much for a jaysus
haah?'

Overheard by Anonymous, under Clery's clock
Posted on Tuesday, 30 May 2006

High-pressure job?

In a busy furniture shop in Liffey Valley the other
day. One of the sales guys was rushing past me
when I said to him, 'Under pressure, yeah?'

To which he replied, with a smile on his face,

'Son, pressure is only for tyres!'

Overheard by Adrian, Liffey Valley
Posted on Tuesday, 30 May 2006

Decent boss

We have quite a 'hands on' boss — Pat. He has
no problem taking over from a worker if they
need a break etc.

One day the phone rang, and it was a customer
looking for the boss. I put them on hold and
asked a few of the factory boys who were in my
office, 'Any sign of Pat?'

They told me he was out in the factory giving

one of the lads a break. So I pick up the phone and said (still can't believe I said this!),

'I'm afraid he's out on the floor, relieving one of the Polish boys!'

Overheard by Anonymous, at work
Posted on Thursday, 25 May 2006

Child protection services, anyone?

A guy at work asking one of the office cleaners about her Spanish holiday:

'So was it any good?'

'Oh yeah, it was brilliant, out on the piss every night until five, and English breakfasts every morning.'

'And did you get a babysitter?'

'Ah no — the child was out with us too — she wouldn't go home!'

Overheard by Anonymous, at work
Posted on Thursday, 25 May 2006

There's always some Anto in the crowd

I was at a Celtic supporters' club meeting a couple of years ago and the Chairman warned us not to leave our belongings on the buses outside Parkhead, because recently the buses were getting robbed during the game.

A couple of issues later the Chairman announced, 'The little nuns of Glasgow are no longer making charitable fund-raisers at Parkhead.'

Some headcase in the crowd called Anto shouts out,

'They don't have to — they're robbing the f**kin' buses!'

Overheard by B, Fraziers, O'Connell Street
Posted on Thursday, 25 May 2006

Give up the day job!

Getting a taxi from Dublin Airport one night and I was half-listening to something on the radio about fighting between India and Pakistan over Kashmir.

The cabbie looks back at me and goes, 'The Indians are on the warpath again, wha?'

Comedy genius!

Overheard by Johnno, cab from the airport
Posted on Sunday, 21 May 2006

What sport is that?

On the DART through Sandymount one day and there is a group of girls playing hockey in the grounds there. An American boy behind me asks,

Boy: 'Mommy, what sport is that?'

Mom: 'I dunno, Sweety, it looks kinda like ice-hockey outside.'

Dad: 'It's called Gaelic soccer …'

Overheard by Liam, on the DART
Posted on Saturday, 20 May 2006

How does milk come out of those?

Little boy, approx. seven years old, in the women's changing rooms in the gym, says to his mother, 'How does milk come out of those?'

To which the mother replies, 'Oh, it's when you have a baby,' and leaves it at that.

The child then laughs and says out very loud, 'I used to suck on them, haha!'

Overheard by Aoife, Westpoint Gym
Posted on Thursday, 11 May 2006

The cry of the common man

Charity mugger (with the usual dreadlocks): 'Excuse me, sir, do you have a second to talk about Oxfam?'

Guy: 'Leave me alone and get a haircut, you hippy!'

Overheard by Jason, Aungier Street
Posted on Thursday, 11 May 2006

Top priority

Speaking of charity muggers …

Chugger: 'Excuse me, could I just ask you for a minute of your time please to talk to you about …'

Guy: 'I'm sorry but I really need to do a poo.'

Chugger just stands there, speechless …

Overheard by Andy, outside Stephen's Green Shopping Centre
Posted on Thursday, 11 May 2006

Vegetarian friendly?

I was in a chipper with my friend, both of us being vegetarians, and she asks the Chinese guy behind the counter,

'Are spice burgers suitable for vegetarians?' and the guy goes,

'Well, there's not MUCH meat in them, it's mainly fat and other shite, so they're kind of vegetarian!'

Overheard by voodoogirl, chipper in Bray
Posted on Thursday, 11 May 2006

Chelsea who?

On the no. 46A bus recently surrounded by noisy D4 boys and girls. I overhear a guy slagging his friend (who was obviously a Man United fan).

Guy: 'Ha ha! Chelsea won!'

On hearing this one of the girls says, 'What, the X Factor?'

Overheard by Anonymous, on the no. 46A bus
Posted on Thursday, 11 May 2006

Excuse me

I was on the Luas the other day, getting off at Heuston Station, very busy, rush hour. Anyway I was making my way through the packed-out Luas, saying 'Excuse me please' etc., when this 'howya' girl shouts all over the place,

'Will yis move outta da f**kin' way, da young

one is tryin to get da hell outta here, now
F**KING MOVE!'

Well, I was 'scarlet'.

Overheard by Kayla, on the Luas
Posted on Wednesday, 10 May 2006

The eccentrics

Upstairs on the no. 150 bus home from town
one evening about seven o'clock, and these two
lads in overalls, half-pissed on the back seat,
were quite loudly fighting over a can of Bud.
Finally they settled down and still quite audibly
began leafing through the *Star* newspaper
together, when one of them pipes up,

'What's this bleedin' word here? Egg-sentrick?'

His mate replies, 'Eccentric, ye bleedin' dope ye,
it's eccentric ... (dramatic, pensive pause) well it
kinda means you're a bit strange and ye do all
sortsa mad stuff. Like yerman Richard Branson
going around the world in a bleedin' balloon
and all that shite. He'd be an eccentric. Ye have
to be rich to be an eccentric, though. If I went
around like that they'd just say I was a mad eejit
and I was crazy ... (further philosophical pause
for effect). Yeah, that's it. If you're rich you're
eccentric, if you're poor — you're just crazy ...'

Overheard by Shane, on the no. 150 bus
Posted on Monday, 8 May 2006

A Dub in a London college

A professor to student, explaining the double
negative:

'… and nowhere in the English language does a double positive mean a negative …'

To which a Dub voice at the back of the lecture room pipes up,

'Yea … right …'

Overheard by BC, a Dub in a London college
Posted on Monday, 8 May 2006

Free Fanta

Me and a few friends were walking around Dun Laoghaire recently. We heard rumours that there were free bottles of Fanta being given out as part of a promotion, but we didn't know where.

While searching for the free Fanta around the streets of Dun Laoghaire, a typical auld fella runs across the road towards us, grabs me by the arm and says,

'Do yez want free drink?' (opens a Superquinn bag with about 30 bottles of Fanta) 'They're given dem out down there.'

Overheard by Hoop, Dun Laoghaire
Posted on Saturday, 6 May 2006

Gambling problem?

I was walking home from the pub one night when a mother ran to catch up with her teenage daughter.

Mother: 'Mary, I've got your jacket here, why the f**k are there betting slips in the pocket, you stupid cow, you must be spending a grand a week in that f**king bookies!'

Mary (not missing a beat and screaming): 'That's not me f**king jacket, ya eijit, you f**king lost me bleeding coat!'

Overheard by Antoinette, in town
Posted on Thursday, 4 May 2006

Mackerel-economics

Before I started college, I got a letter from the college with a list of the subjects I would be studying, one of which was Macroeconomics. I was in the kitchen talking to my Mom and said, 'What's Macroeconomics?'

At which point my Dad came in, a wee bit drunk from the pub and shouts,

'Sure mackerel's a bleedin' fish.'

Right so, Dad.

Overheard by Voodoogirl, in my kitchen
Posted on Tuesday, 2 May 2006

Tongue-tied

Standing at a bus stop on the South Circular, I happened to notice a young couple kissing with

a degree of passion, but not what you'd call X-rated by any means, when a guy cycles past with a friendly,

'Get your f**king tongue out of her mouth!'

And they say romance is dead?

Overheard by Deebs, South Circular Road
Posted on Sunday, 30 April 2006

Gender bending in Inchicore

I used to get my hair cut in this very old-fashioned barber shop in Inchicore. I'm in there one afternoon — there's only me, the barber, a couple of auld fellas and a young mother with two sons. The black and white movie that was on telly finishes up, and Shirley Temple Bar comes on screen with the bingo numbers.

This causes a certain amount of discomfort with the auld fellas. They mutter a bit but the TV stays on. Then one of the young kids asks his Mammy, 'Mammy, is that a man or a woman on TV?'

His mother replies, 'It's a f**kin' eejit is what it is.'

Overheard by Baz, Inchicore
Posted on Saturday, 29 April 2006

Dancing sparks?

Seen this written in a toilet on a building site. Being a sparky myself, found it funny:

'Here come all the sparkys, dressed as ballroom dancers,

One in ten is qualified, the rest are f**in' chancers!'

Overheard by Ric, building site, Dublin
Posted on Tuesday, 25 April 2006

More than he bargained for!

In Busaras the other day, in one of the shops. A young guy queuing in front of me had ordered a cup of tea with milk and no sugar. The foreign girl behind the counter asked him,

'Would you like your bag squeezed?'

The guy replies,

'No, I'll just have the tea.'

He managed to keep a straight face — unlike myself who had to leave the shop!

Overheard by Stephen, shop in Busaras
Posted on Monday, 24 April 2006

Oh, suits you!

I overheard two gay guys on Georges Street (where else?). One was admiring the other's jacket.

Gay guy #1: 'I love your jacket, what make is it?'

Gay guy #2: 'Gucci.'

Gay guy #1: 'Oh! Gucci, Gucci, Goo!'

Overheard by Anonymous, Georges Street
Posted on Monday, 24 April 2006

Health health health!

In a Spar in the Liberties, mum with screaming brat:

Child: 'Ma, Ma, I want crisps … crisps, Ma … I want some crisps … crisps … crisps, Ma!'

Mother: 'No! You're not getting crisps, they're bad for you.'

Shopkeeper: 'Can I help you?'

Mother: 'Ten Marlboro Lights, please.'

Overheard by Paul, Spar

Posted on Friday, 21 April 2006

Leinster fans …

I was queuing last Friday at Donnybrook for tickets for the Leinster versus Munster match. My friend came over to keep me company, and the guy behind me asked my friend if he was going to the match.

He said no, he wasn't all that interested in rugby, and if he went he'd probably spend the time reading the newspaper, listening to his i-Pod and texting his mates. The guy behind said,

'Ah, you'd fit right in, so.'

Overheard by Anonymous, Donnybrook

Posted on Thursday, 20 April 2006

Inappropriate!

At a 5-a-side soccer tournament in UCD a few weeks ago, great craic. Afterwards, the referee declares, 'That was great, lads, I haven't had as much fun since I buried the mother-in-law ...'

Overheard by Louise, UCD
Posted on Thursday, 20 April 2006

Senior Cup

I was on the no. 46A bus on the way out of town. A bunch of lads from Blackrock get on at RTÉ. They started talking about their school rugby team and how they were playing in the middle of the mocks.

Jock #1: 'It's so unfair that they're expected to play in the middle of their mocks.'

Jock #2: 'I know, you'd think they'd move the mocks. You can always repeat the Leaving — you only get one shot at the Senior Cup.'

Overheard by Mick, on the no. 46A bus
Posted on Thursday, 20 April 2006

Interracial bonding

About 2 a.m. at the late-night window of a Texaco garage in Blackrock. Scumbag gets out of a van and waddles up to the window. There is an Asian man working there. The scumbag then roars aggressively at him in his best Asian accent,

'CHING BA PHAN DOO WAH' ... followed by ... 'DOES DAT MEAN ANYTIN' TO YOU, DUZ IH?'

Overheard by Rob, Texaco garage, Blackrock
Posted on Thursday, 20 April 2006

In the chipper

Standing in a chipper waiting for my order and a bloke walks in and orders the following:

'Will ye give us a bag of chips and two sausages and will you batter the f**k out of them for me, cheers?'

Overheard by Rob, chipper in Palmerstown
Posted on Thursday, 20 April 2006

All tracksuits are the same

Woman holds up two Reebok tracksuit tops and goes to her husband, 'Which one do you prefer?'

He says back to her, 'Don't take offence, love, but they all look the f**king same when they're on ya.'

So true. So true.

Overheard by Alan, Lifestyle Sports, Ilac Centre
Posted on Thursday, 20 April 2006

Brave eejit

Sitting on the no. 13A bus to Ballymun on Thursday surrounded by snivelling junkies and wreathed in clouds of hash smoke. Well-dressed gent beside me answers mobile phone and wife asks where he is:

'I'm on the skanger ride from hell,' he says, without batting an eyelid.

Overheard by a 13A victim, on the no. 13A bus
Posted on Wednesday, 19 April 2006

Confused?!

I was working at the information desk when a little boy about age three came up to my work colleague, looking lost, and asked her,

'Have you seen a woman going around without a boy that looks like me?'

Overheard by Beth, Shankill Shopping Centre
Posted on Wednesday, 19 April 2006

Music to watch the girls go by

Picture this. It's Tallaght, da boyz are in their car, blaring the tunes, rippin' around the estate like a dog on fire, shades on (even though it's nearing dark), equipped with those reflective blue light thingys that racer boys have under their set of wheels, beeping at anything in a skirt, about six fellas roaring, 'Wahey, luv, show us yer tits,' to every passing girl under the age of 30.

But there's something not right. Whilst I was waiting for my bus, they circled the estate several times, blaring one tune on repeat. It's not Scooter, it's not DJ Quicksilver … it's …

Shania Twain, 'Man, I feel like a woman' …

Overheard by M, Tallaght
Posted on Tuesday, 18 April 2006

You'd either love it or hate it

Was at the UCI Cinema in Coolock with a few mates last weekend and we asked the cashier guy about the films that had just started. We asked about one film in particular, to see if it was worth watching, and his reply was …

'I actually just saw it last night, it's a film you either love or hate. I thought it was alright.'

Overheard by ILLB, UCI Cinema Coolock
Posted on Tuesday, 18 April 2006

Hot stuff

Was in the Northside Shopping Centre looking for a present for my brother when I heard two oul' ones talking about a lava lamp:

Lady #1: 'Look at da, wharisit?'

Lady #2: 'It's a lava lamp.'

Lady #1 (touching it): 'It's very warm!'

Lady #2: 'Course it is, there's lava in it!'

Overheard by Kevin K, Northside Shopping Centre
Posted on Tuesday, 18 April 2006

Like mother, like son

My friend accompanies his father on a shopping trip for his Mum's birthday. While in a lingerie shop, the assistant asks the father if she can help. After some general questions, the assistant asks the father what size he is buying for. The father turns to his son (my pal) and loudly asks,

'Colin, what size are you?'

Overheard by Pocket Rocket, from my friend
Posted on Monday, 17 April 2006

Yes, no, Coke ...

Standing behind a woman in line for KFC. She orders (along with other stuff) a 'Coke'. The young Asian clerk behind the counter replies, 'I am sorry, we have no Coke.'

Woman: 'You have no Coke?'

Asian clerk: 'Yes.'

Woman: 'So you've got Coke?'

Asian clerk: 'No, we have no Coke.'

Woman: 'You have no Coke?'

Asian clerk: 'Yes.'

Woman: 'So you've got Coke?'

Overheard by Lamont, KFC at Clare Hall
Posted on Monday, 17 April 2006

The beautiful accent

Behind a group of French kids in McDonald's on Grafton Street. They pool their money together, and the best English-speaker is chosen to go to the counter and put the order in.

'Three Big Mac meals and two McChicken sandwiches, please,' says the chosen kid.

'Is dah ih?' replies the girl on the counter.

The French kid looks confused.

'Three Big Mac meals and two Mc ...'

'Yeah, I've got dat. Is dah it? Anyting else?'

After some chattering amongst themselves, they

just hand her a bunch of money and stare at her, bemused.

Overheard by Rory, McDonald's, Grafton Street
Posted on Monday, 17 April 2006

Colours, sizes, locations ... all too much!

Staff guy at Tan.ie serving some girl.

Guy: 'OK, nine minutes. You're in room no. 2, just press the blue button on the wall when you're ready to start the sunbed.'

Gal: 'Wha?'

Guy: 'When you're ready to start the sunbed, just press the blue button on the wall.'

Gal: 'Awwwwwww, right.'

Few minutes later she emerges from the tanning rooms:

Gal (shouting): 'It didn't come on!'

Guy goes in and checks while Gal stands in shop, bitching about why it's all a scam.

Guy emerges from rooms:

'It didn't start 'cos instead of pressing the Small Blue Button on the wall labelled "Start", you pressed the Large Red Button on the inside of the bed labelled "Emergency Stop".'

Overheard by Justin, Tan.ie (Chartbusters) in Clare Hall
Posted on Sunday, 16 April 2006

Rear 'em right

An auld granny pushing the young wan's baby in the pram. Granny leans over and goo-es at the baby and says, 'Giv us a luv!'

Baby gurgles. Encouraged, Granny leans in again and with a little more enthusiasm says, 'Ah gwan, giv us a luv!'

Baby beams responsively, Granny gets into the moment, leans over again, tickles baby and says, 'Ah, gwan, giv' us a f**kin' luv!'

Overheard by Wu, Irish Life Mall off Talbot Street
Posted on Sunday, 16 April 2006

Politically incorrect

Late 1990s and a few mates of mine were working as security guards on the door of shops on Grafton Street, watching out for shop-lifters. As you know, security guards have their own lingo for most things.

My mate on radio: 'Jim, there's a few knackers gone into Monsoon.'

Controller to all units: 'For the last time, lads, don't be calling them knackers, we could get into trouble for that.'

My mate: 'Right, Bud. Jim, there's a few cream crackers gone into Monsoon.'

Overheard by John, Grafton Street
Posted on Sunday, 16 April 2006

Has it all except Irish Times

A guy goes up to the newsagent counter and the girl behind it asks, 'What do you want?'

He replies, 'Thanks to a good education and wealthy parents, I want for nothing, however I do require a copy of the *Irish Times*.'

Overheard by Derrick, at a shop beside the Four Courts
Posted on Saturday, 15 April 2006

The auld ones

Old Lady #1: 'Did you hear what happened to Bernie yesterday morning after mass?'

Old Lady #2: 'Someone told me she took sick …'

Old Lady #1: 'Mmmm. Got up and ran straight to the vestry after the communion.'

Old Lady #2: 'My God, what was wrong with her?'

Old Lady #1: 'Coleslaw!' (followed by a knowing sniff)

Old Lady #2: 'Oh no! That happened to me before.'

Old Lady #1: 'Mmmm, yes.'

Old Lady# 2: 'Mmmm, coleslaw, yes. It's lethal.'

Overheard by Liz, on the DART passing through Killester
Posted on Saturday, 15 April 2006

If ignorance is bliss, then meet the happiest girl in the world

In school, one of my nearest and dearest friends was telling us about the Ireland match she and her boyfriend had been to see the night before. We all asked her how it was and did she have a good time, to which she replied,

'I enjoyed it an' all but I was lost in the second half.'

I asked her why? Her answer was,

'Well, the gobshites changed sides.'

Overheard by Toni, Dublin school
Posted on Friday, 14 April 2006

Paying for a good education

While observing a case in the Four Courts last year. The girl in question was a past pupil of a well-known large south-Dublin fee-paying school.

Defence barrister: 'Is this where you were residing at the time?'

Girl: 'Sorry, what do you mean by residing?'

Her parents must be so proud — that was money well spent!

Overheard by observer, Court 24, the Four Courts

Posted on Friday, 14 April 2006

Buttered up by an Asian girl

I asked the Asian-looking girl behind the deli counter for a roll with sausages, rashers and tomato ketchup. As the girl replied too quickly and loudly for my ears to discern what she was saying, I asked her to repeat herself again and again and again.

Still unable to make out what she was asking me after her third attempt to communicate with me, I thought she was going to flip when she took a few deep breaths, composed herself and said:

'BUH ER? D'ya want Buh er on yar roll?' in the thickest Dublin accent imaginable. I said yes and thanked her very much. I left smiling to myself — completely forgetting to pay for the roll!

Overheard by Aidan, Spar

Posted on Thursday, 13 April 2006

Maxin' relaxin'

I was in a hospital the other day when I heard this guy from the next room shouting for ages. He then screamed, 'Oh God, somebody help me!'

I told a nurse that was walking by and she just said, 'He's crazy.'

Two minutes later a doctor went in to calm the man down.

Doctor: 'Would you relax?'

Patient: 'I'm gonna f**king relax your head against the wall in a minute.'

Overheard by Sean, St James's Hospital
Posted on Wednesday, 12 April 2006

Multi-talented George Foreman

I was watching the film *Ali* with my girlfriend and it came to the 'Rumble in the Jungle' between Muhammad Ali and George Foreman. Bear in mind this was a documentary of Ali's life.

Ring announcer: 'In the left corner we have George Foreman!'

Girlfriend: 'Oh my God, I can't believe he is an actor *and* a chef!'

Overheard by Niall, Star Century
Posted on Wednesday, 12 April 2006

Kids in the pub

We were just after leaving a pub on Paddy's Day that was full of kids watching their parents getting rubbered. So we got talking about how much of a waste of a day it was to have the kids locked up in a pub.

Heading home we jumped in a taxi. The taxi driver was full of chat and was asking about what we'd done for the day.

One of the lads — for the craic — says, 'Ah, nothing better then bringing the kids to the pub and having a few pints on Paddy's Day,' and the taxi driver goes,

'Ah God yeah, you're right, sure I was there this morning with them.'

Overheard by Deco, in a Dublin taxi

Posted on Tuesday, 11 April 2006

Half price!

Walking down the road, man on push bike with Tesco bags. The man just cycling, minding his own business, when a car slows down by him, window rolls down, and girl with a doll in her hands holds the doll out, screams out, 'HALF PRICE AT TESCO …'

Only in Dublin!

Overheard by Anonymous, city centre

Posted on Tuesday, 11 April 2006

Wear them and die?

Old dear (dealer) on Henry Street: 'Get the last of the Terminal underwear!'

Overheard by Wally, Henry Street

Posted on Tuesday, 11 April 2006

Not the sharpest tool in the box

In Superquinn in Walkinstown last night. I was at the checkout and the checkout girl says, 'If any of you have less than five items you can go to the checkout at the off-licence.'

A woman behind me with one item in her hand (big piece of meat) says to me,

'I have less than five items, don't I?'

Overheard by Mossy, Superquinn, Walkinstown
Posted on Monday, 10 April 2006

Politically unaware

On the no. 42 bus to Malahide, couple of young ones. Passing by a house:

Young one #1: 'That's Charlie Haughey's house.'

Young one #2: 'Who's he?'

Young one #1: 'You're a bleedin' thick, sure wasn't he the President of Ireland.'

Overheard by Barry, on the no. 42 bus
Posted on Monday, 10 April 2006

Skangers versus D4s

Was coming out of Dundrum Shopping Centre on Saturday, three D4 head girls walking towards me (with the quiffed hairs and the UGG boots).

There was a gang of skangers sitting on the wall at the fountain, and one of them wolf-whistled over at the girls. They giggled and turned around to soak up the praise, but to their obvious dismay, the whistling skanger shouted,

'Wasn't wistlin' at yous, yiz uglee bitches!'

All the skangers fell about the place laughing … class.

Overheard by David, Dundrum Shopping Centre
Posted on Monday, 10 April 2006

Coming off bread

Two sales assistants discussing what to get for their lunch. The first girl says to her mate, 'I'm trying to give up bread, it's bad for me.'

The second girl replies, 'Yer dead right, I was reading the ingredients on a packet of bread the other day, it's full of bleeding addictives!'

Overheard by Sinéad, clothes shop
Posted on Sunday, 9 April 2006

I had to ask!

I was waiting for the bus from Busáras to go to the airport, but the CityLink bus which is supposed to be very regular hadn't appeared in over 30 minutes. When I eventually got on the bus I raised my voice over the traffic to ask the bus driver,

'How regular are you?' — no sooner had I said it I knew it came out wrong — to which he replied,

'At least once a day!'

Overheard by KL, Busáras
Posted on Sunday, 9 April 2006

Hail to the bus driver

Getting on the no. 46A bus heading towards town. Pulling change out of my pocket for fare. I had €1.10 and a €2 coin. The fare was €1.05. I popped the €2 coin into the machine. The driver looks at me and says,

'This isn't a savin' scheme I'm running here!'

Overheard by Stebag, on the no. 46A bus

Posted on Sunday, 9 April 2006

Begging techniques

Was walking towards Grafton Street when this old homeless lad shouts out, 'Here! Give us some money or I'll give ya a box!'

I turned round to see him standing there with a cardboard box in his hand — and a big smile on his face. Had to give him some cash after that …

Overheard by Kev, St Stephen's Green

Posted on Saturday, 8 April 2006

Classy

Couple in their 40s get on the bus and she goes upstairs. He asks the driver for change of €20, and then holds up the whole bus, arguing with the driver that he hasn't any more money.

From upstairs you hear her shouting, 'Darren, will ye hurry up!'

Next she shouts, 'If I hafta come downstayers there is gonna be some amount of trouble.'

Then you hear her stomping downstairs, screaming at the bus driver, 'I'm f**kin' disabled. I'm f**kin' disabled. What's your problem, it's not coming out of your bleedin' pockeh!'

She then grabs the man and storms back upstairs, still shouting at the driver.

At Cork Street she screams again, 'Get your bleedin' hands off me,' stomps downstairs again, smoking a smoke, gets off — and lies down by the railings!

Overheard by Sarah, on the no. 77A bus

Posted on Saturday, 8 April 2006

Erectile dysfunction

A good-looking girl was walking ahead of me through town. We were passing a building covered with scaffolding. One of the workers was leaning against the scaffold near the path. He winks at the girl as she passes, sweeps out a dramatic hand gesture towards the scaffold and says,

'Wha de ye tink o' me massive erection, love?'

Nice!

Overheard by Anonymous, Mercer Street

Posted on Saturday, 8 April 2006

Spare change

I was queuing for the ATM on Grafton Street one night, and as per usual there was a beggar, sitting in between both machines, sure to get some attention.

Beggar: 'Hey mista, any spare change, pleeaaasss?'

Me: 'Sorry man, all I have is a fifty.'

Beggar: 'No worries, I'll give ya change!'

Overheard by Peter, Grafton Street

Posted on Friday, 7 April 2006

Prazky: crazy-old-drunk-approved

At Ranelagh Luas stop there was this old drunk sort of talking to himself. I was carrying a six-pack of Prazky. Suddenly the old drunk shouts at me, with much enthusiasm,

'Prazky! By God, that's the way to do it, boy!'

Overheard by Dan, Ranelagh Luas stop
Posted on Friday, 7 April 2006

ALLIGATOR

Walking through Temple Bar last Saturday, I noticed a bit of a commotion and headed towards it. Two lads appeared to be in a bit of a scrap and the Garda asks one of the lads, 'What are the allegations you are making?'

To which the man replies, 'No, he's the alligator (pointing toward other lad) …'

FACT!

Overheard by Andy, Temple Bar
Posted on Friday, 7 April 2006

Telling it as it is

On the Luas last night just before the stop for Heuston Station, all of a sudden the driver slams the brakes and we screech to a halt, cue shrieks and general confusion as everyone thought we had crashed. The driver then switches on the intercom and announces ever so politely,

'Sorry about that, ladies and gents, some GOBSHITE just ran a red light right in front of us!'

Overheard by Ciara, Luas Red Line
Posted on Friday, 7 April 2006

Who's driving who?

On the no. 4 bus to Ballymun.

Bus stops at the top of Parnell Square, driver sticks his head out and shouts down the bus at the passengers,

'Any a youz use dis route regular? How do I get to Phibsboro from here?'

Everyone just laughs and wonders if they'll make it home at all!

Overheard by Anonymous, no. 4 bus to Ballymun
Posted on Friday, 7 April 2006

Discourage them while they're young

I was in the Ilac Centre Library and there was a mother in there with her young child. The child picks up a book and starts looking at it. The mum yells,

'PUT THAT BOOK DOWN, YOU KNOW YOU
CAN'T READ!

What encouragement …

Overheard by Anna, Ilac Centre Central Library
Posted on Thursday, 6 April 2006

Blondie & Blondie

Two quite pretty blonde girls (around 19) sitting
in the ground floor café in the Jervis Centre,
talking (I thought) about the Iraq war. One (the
one wearing a pink hoody amazingly) says, 'It's
so terrible about Iraq,' to which the other
replies,

'Oh my God, I know, the dust storms are awful
there, women have to cover their heads so their
hair doesn't get ruined …'

Overheard by Rick, in the ground floor café of the Jervis Centre
Posted on Thursday, 6 April 2006

Disgusting!

I was in Barcode on Paddy's Night and my friend
and I went to use the ladies. As we made our
way to the toilets we passed a group of lads
playing pool. On our way back from the ladies
one of the lads yells,

'I would have loved to be the toilet seat you two
sat on!'

Overheard by K, Barcode
Posted on Thursday, 6 April 2006

Sound advice

While standing in a queue in a shop on South Circular Road I overheard a D4 girl ask for a cylinder of gas. She then asked,

'Like, how long will this bottle of gas last?' to which the shopkeeper quickly answered,

'Well, darling, if you never turn the cooker on it will last forever!'

Overheard by Gerry, shop, South Circular Road
Posted on Thursday, 6 April 2006

Shamrock shake

I was near Christ Church with my friends from America who were sampling a Shamrock Shake, which of course comes out around Paddy's Day every year.

A courier is cycling by quite fast and somehow spots the milkshake in my hand. As he cycles off into the distance he shouts back in a thick Dublin accent,

'Here, Bud, is that a Shamrock Shake?', to which I shout back, 'Yeah.' Courier shouts back enthusiastically from the distance, 'NICE ONE!'

Overheard by Dara, Christ Church
Posted on Wednesday, 5 April 2006

Paddy's Night mayhem

'I've lost the will to live.'

A clearly fed-up Garda expressing his feelings to another Garda.

Overheard by Fiona, in Temple Bar on Paddy's Night
Posted on Wednesday, 5 April 2006

Thick as thieves

Two blokes outside Paddy Powers having a smoke; one was asking the other if he knew 'John', to which the other replied,

'Of course I do, I've done loads of robberies with him.'

Overheard by Anonymous, outside Paddy Powers in Rathmines
Posted on Wednesday, 5 April 2006

Zero tolerance

Stressed out Posh Mother to misbehaving child (about five years old): 'Right, okay, right, that's it, that's final, that's absolutely final. You're getting no new toys and no McDonald's for a WHOLE WEEK.'

Overheard by DB, Tesco, Nutgrove Shopping Centre
Posted on Wednesday, 5 April 2006

Taxi humour

In a taxi with my boyfriend going out to DCU. We're chatting away to the taxi driver and he asks me what I'm studying. So I tell him about my course and he says, 'Ah, dat's great.'

Next thing he turns around, looks at my boyfriend and says, 'Jaysus, what are you studying to be — a heart-throb?'

We were both in hysterics. Yet another example of razor-sharp Dublin taxi driver wit!

Overheard by Dom, taxi
Posted on Wednesday, 5 April 2006

English lessons needed

Walking down Camden Street past two vegetable stalls. At the same time a man in his 20s was walking a bike with a flat tyre past the stalls.

Woman behind stall shouts out: 'Mister, yur chain is flaa!'

Man replies in French accent: 'Excuse me?'

Woman replies: 'I said, yur chain is flaa!'

French man replies: 'I do not understand.'

Woman behind stall replies: 'Ahh, come back to me when you learn English.'

Overheard by Anonymous, Camden Street
Posted on Tuesday, 4 April 2006

Banguard

I was out for lunch with a girl from work. She is not the brightest spark. She was telling me about a mutual friend who had gotten engaged.

I said, 'Oh yeah, she's marrying a guard, isn't she?'

The dope said, 'No, she's actually marrying a *banguard*.'

Confused, I said, 'Sorry?'

She replied, 'Yeah, he is in the Garda Band —
banguard, see …?'

Overheard by Nicola, Blanchardstown

Posted on Tuesday, 4 April 2006

A culchie thing to do

I was on the Luas Green Line going from St
Stephen's Green, and suddenly this old man
reeking of gin pushes in beside me on the seat.
As soon as he did this, he turned to me, scanned
me with his eyes and goes, 'You a culchie?'

I just said no, and started listening to some
music.

When the Luas stopped in Beechwood, a black
man tried to bring a bicycle onto the Luas, and
immediately the driver announces that he wasn't
allowed to bring a bike on the Luas. The old
man looks back, tuts at the black man, then
turns to me and goes,

'A bike on the Luas … that's a real culchie thing
to do.'

Overheard by Cian, on the Luas, Beechwood Station.

Posted on Tuesday, 4 April 2006

Fashion statement

Nice-looking girl wearing a t-shirt with a pair of
eyes printed across the chest, walks by a group
of road workers in yellow jackets.

On cue, one of them says, 'Nice eyes!'

Overheard by Robbo, Pearse Street

Posted on Monday, 3 April 2006

Dangerous woman

My brother had a bit of heartburn and was asking some people at work if they had anything for it. A nice older woman kindly assists, looking through her handbag of drugs saying, 'I have some of that semtex in here.'

Think she meant Zantac …

Overheard by Anonymous, workplace
Posted on Monday, 3 April 2006

In touch with his inner self

Some years ago, I was walking along near Stephen's Green on a gorgeous, sunny summer morning. It seemed that everyone was out enjoying the day. The street was fairly crowded with women pushing prams, school-kids, a bit of everything.

To one side of the path, there was a huge pile of Bord Gáis, bright, canary-yellow PVC pipes, piled in a pyramid about 6 foot high, about to be installed somewhere nearby. There must have been over a hundred of them, and they really were striking in their 'yellowness'.

Of course, a crowded Dublin street would not be complete without the friendly neighbourhood nutter, and sure enough, one came bouncing along, talking to himself.

When he came within view of the pipes, he froze and suddenly started shouting at the top of his lungs,

'YELLOW! YELLOW! YELLOW!'

Overheard by Heather, near St Stephen's Green
Posted on Sunday, 2 April 2006

He's right!

An old drunk, sitting singing on the bus, glared out at a billboard for 7 Up Free and shouted, 'F**king sham — 7 Up's not free!'

We were all in stitches ...

Overheard by Paul, the no. 130 bus coming home from town
Posted on Sunday, 2 April 2006

Getting out

Was out in the Red Cow Hotel playing a poker tournament recently, and during a break I had the following conversation with a true Dub:

Me: 'I've seen you at every poker tournament I've been at lately, do you ever not play, you know take a break?'

Guy: 'Do you ever wonder why I play so much?'

Me: 'You're making money!?'

Guy: 'No it's not that, but if you saw the mutt I had waiting for me at home you'd get out of the house as often as you could too.'

Overheard by Patrick, Red Cow Hotel

Posted on Saturday, 1 April 2006

Immaculate contraception

At the no. 77 bus stop, two youngish girls, maybe sixteen years old, discussing the contraceptive implant:

'It's like a match stick, goes under your skin, don't protect you from dem STDs though.'

'Wha abou' STIs?'

'What's dem then?'

'You know, a sexually transmitted injury?'

Overheard by Anonymous, at the no. 77 bus stop

Posted on Saturday, 1 April 2006

Where'll I meet ya so?

Walking out from Irish Life on Abbey Street for my lunch break and pass by a young yobbo with a phone glued to his ear, yammering away, trying to meet up with his friend. It went something like this:

Yob: 'Yeah, I'm outside Irish … eh? … Roight I'm on Abbey … F**k! Roight! You know the Spire? Grand, cause I'm nowhere near tha!'

Overheard by John, Abbey Street

Posted on Saturday, 1 April 2006

The invisible car

After leaving the Dew Drop in Kill slightly worse for wear, we walked down the road towards my sister's boyfriend's house. After a few minutes a Garda car pulls up beside them. The window rolls down.

Garda: 'Are you driving?'

Well …

Overheard by Ian, Kill (near Dublin)
Posted on Saturday, 1 April 2006

Good observation

While walking through the Square in Tallaght, I noticed two Tallaghites standing at the top of an escalator which wasn't moving. They were staring in bemusement at the motionless stairway, when after a good few minutes one looked up and said,

'I think we're going to have to walk.'

Overheard by Pete, Tallaght Square
Posted on Wednesday, 29 March 2006

From the mouths of babes …

We all know how small children can REALLY embarrass adults, but this to me took the biscuit.

Little girl in the checkout queue was throwing a mega tantrum because Mammy wouldn't buy her sweets. When screaming, shouting, crying, lying on the floor and kicking didn't achieve the desired result, she stood, drew herself up to her full height, and yelled at the top of her voice,

'I saw you kissing Daddy's willie!'

I needn't tell you that one VERY embarrassed
mother dropped her shopping and fled! I'm still
laughing about it a year later!

Overheard by Anonymous, Tesco, The Square, Tallaght
Posted on Wednesday, 29 March 2006

Hmmm bop! or bus?!?

On the no. 16 to Rathfarnham when the bus
pulls up at a stop. Three D4 young rugger heads
that look like Hanson (remember them?)
wannabes are standing half on/half off the bus
debating something, when the bus driver vents
his rage at them:

'Come on, girls, will ye?!'

The Hanson boys started blushing and the bus
started laughing …

Overheard by Chops, on the no. 16 bus
Posted on Wednesday, 29 March 2006

Fag area?

Was at a gay night out a few years ago with a
male friend. We decided to go out for a smoke,
and my friend (who is wearing a dress, stilettos,
wig and makeup) asks the bouncer,

'D'ya know where the fag area is?'

Poor bouncer was still laughing when we passed
him ten minutes later …

Overheard by Annette, the Ambassador
Posted on Wednesday, 29 March 2006

Canal rescue

Along the canal at Baggot Street, a guy running past had managed to fall in. A large crowd gathered to watch the rescue operation which involved about 30 policemen, an ambulance, a rescue unit and two fire brigades.

The attempt to get him out using a rope had failed because he had pulled it in on top of himself, so they lowered a ladder. For some reason the (stoned or drunk) guy in the water swam around the back of the ladder and was screaming, 'Ouch me legs, me legs are freezing!'

At this stage the fireman lost his temper and shouted down, 'Shut up moanin' and climb up the ladder, ya f**kin' eejit!'

We were all thinking it!

Overheard by Stacy, Grand Canal at Baggot Street
Posted on Tuesday, 28 March 2006

A1 maths student?

On the bus home from work and a trio of secondary students pile on to an already packed bus. Their conversation is about their impending Leaving Cert exams this summer and one of the girls exclaims, 'I sooo need to get an A1 in maths to get my course.'

The conversation continues and then leads to talk of their mocks in April which prompts one of the girls to wonder how long they had 'til then. The A1 student pipes up,

'Don't worry that's, like, 20 weeks away.'

Overheard by AMB, on the no. 41 bus
Posted on Tuesday, 28 March 2006

Jim Apple

In Dubray Books in Dun Laoghaire I overheard a
secondary school student enquiring about a
school book at the desk. 'Do you have Jim
Apple?'

'Jim Apple?' the confused clerk replied.

'Yeah, Jim Apple, it's a French book,' answered
the teen.

'Oh, *Je m'appelle*,' the clerk replied, holding
back a smirk. 'I'll just get it for you now.'

Let's hope there's a chapter in that book on
pronunciation.

Overheard by Jack, Dubray Bookshop, Dun Laoghaire
Posted on Tuesday, 28 March 2006

Who needs the FBI

A while ago I was watching *Crimeline* on RTÉ
and one of our finest was going through the
details of a robbery that took place. He picks up
a small green petrol tank and the rest goes like
this.

Presenter: 'What's that you've got there?'

Garda: 'It's a green petrol container found at the
crime scene and we believe it was used to carry
petrol.'

I know you're thinking: 'Made up.'

I wish it was …

Overheard by Jimmy, *Crimeline*, RTÉ TV (Donnybrook)
Posted on Monday, 27 March 2006

Bulimic ... classic Dublin!

While out walking my dog a couple of months ago I passed a group of early teens talking about and getting ready for the upcoming night's merriments. One lad in particular was at one of the girls to come out and get trolleyed with them.

He pestered her until she got annoyed and gave the definitive answer:

'I told ye no! If me Ma catches me drinking again she'll go bulimic!'

Overheard by Will, Dundrum
Posted on Monday, 27 March 2006

Fashion police

I was in a sports shop last week in my civies when some aul' one taps me on the shoulder. As I turn around she barks, 'Size five, love, I'm in a rush,' to which I reply, 'Sorry I don't work here.'

Instead of her walking away rather sheepishly, she shouts, 'What, you mean they're your normal clothes? You're mad!'

Overheard by Roger Le Mont, The Square
Posted on Monday, 27 March 2006

Irish v. Germans

Guy on the bus asks for the fare *as Gaeilge*.

Bus driver (in a thick Dub accent): 'Nie sprecken de Irish.'

Overheard by Tom, on the no. 46A bus
Posted on Monday, 27 March 2006

Urinal traffic management

In the cinema a few months back. Movie ended and the scramble to the gents began. The toilets were crowded, as a number of films ended together, and there was a queue of two or three lads behind each urinal.

Then from the back of the queue, a random man in his best Dublin authoritarian voice shouts:

'Right, lads, have 'em out and ready when approaching the urinal!'

The guys didn't know whether to laugh, or pretend they couldn't hear!

Overheard by P, Savoy Cinema
Posted on Sunday, 26 March 2006

When the customer is a 13-year-old boy

I was at the local Spar, and this 13-year-old was at the counter buying a bottle of Pepsi.

He was counting one, two and five cents out, really slowly, just to annoy the girl behind the counter. When he finally got to the right amount, he threw the rest of the change down, grabbed his bottle and said,

'Keep the change, get yourself a decent haircut.'

He walked out — leaving me and the poor girl speechless!

Overheard by Katelynn, local Spar
Posted on Sunday, 26 March 2006

Good enough excuse as any

Walking along the street I noticed a young man being searched by a guard. Garda said to him,

'I'm arresting you for being a dickhead!'

Only in Ireland …

Overheard by Shauna, beside St Stephen's Green Shopping Centre
Posted on Sunday, 26 March 2006

Beer goggles

My brother and his mate sitting at the bar in their local, where the people within earshot heard the following conversation.

Brother: 'Mick, you're drunk.'

Mick: 'Feck off. What do you mean?'

Brother: 'You're pissed, I can tell when you've had too much.'

Mick: 'Ah stop messing and keep your voice down, you're very loud.'

Brother: 'I'm just telling you the facts, just ask anyone.'

Mick: 'How are you so sure that I'm drunk?'

Brother: 'You're gone all blurred …'

Overheard by Higgs, The Royal Oak
Posted on Saturday, 25 March 2006

Tasty

I was in the queue for breakfast in Jurys Ballsbridge last summer, when these two Yanks came back up for seconds.

'Scuse me, waiter,' she says, 'What are those black things? They were really delicious. We got nothing like that back home. What is it?'

Waiter: 'It's black pudding, very nice.'

'What's it made from?' she asks.

'Pig's blood,' comes the forthright reply.

American gent: 'I think we'll just have the eggs …'

Overheard by Shamo, Jurys Ballsbridge
Posted on Saturday, 25 March 2006

Patriotic pub customer

Elderly patriotic gentleman goes into his local pub much later than usual on a Sunday night about four years ago. He has obviously been drinking.

The barman says, 'Well, Johnny, we've been missing you. Where were you at all?'

'I was at a funeral,' declares Johnny.

'Who's funeral?' asks the barman.

'Kevin Barry's!' shouts Johnny.

'Jaze, I didn't even know he was sick,' replies the barman.

Overheard by Anonymous, Leeson Lounge
Posted on Saturday, 25 March 2006

Medical help

Young girl at bus stop on mobile phone:

Girl: 'I'm in town. Will you meet me?'

'Where are you?'

Girl: 'I'm opposite a shop. It's "The V ..., V ..." '

(Interrupted by man next to her) Man: 'It's the "VHI", love!'

Overheard by Anonymous, it happened to a friend of my daughter
Posted on Friday, 24 March 2006

Blondes

Two young wans sitting behind me on the no. 43 bus, discussing the merits of dyed hair, when one says to the other,

'If I had me hair dyed blonde and I was pregnant, would the baby be blonde too?'

Overheard by Anonymous, on the no. 43 bus
Posted on Friday, 24 March 2006

Surely there was a better place to make this call ...

Picture it: no. 10 bus going home from work the other evening. Young Dublin boy in front of me decides to call some girl that he had obviously only met the previous weekend. Conversation goes something like this:

Dublin Boy: 'Hi, Joanne, it's Danny!'

Girl: 'Danny who?'

Dublin Boy: 'Danny ... remember? The guy from last weekend?'

There's a couple of seconds of a pause:

Dublin Boy: 'Hello? Hello ...?'

She had hung up on him.

Everyone on the bus was in fits of laughter and the red-faced young fella got off at the next stop.

Overheard by Jonathan, on the no. 10 bus

Posted on Friday, 24 March 2006